To Ben
God Bless

WOW!
WHAT A RIDE

MY LIFE AND JOURNEY WITH JERRY FALWELL

DUKE WESTOVER
FOREWORD BY MIKE HUCKABEE

21stCENTURY
P R E S S
READING YOU LOUD AND CLEAR.

WHAT A RIDE

ISBN 978-0-9824428-9-0

Cover: Keith Locke
Book Design: Lee Fredrickson

Visit our website at: www.21stcenturypress.com

2131 W. Republic Rd., PMB 41,
Springfield, MO 65807

21stCENTURY
P R E S S
READING YOU LOUD AND CLEAR.

DEDICATION

This book is dedicated to memories;
memories of 55 wonderful years of marriage,
54 years of being a father and
38 years of having a best friend.

I could never be this lucky and blessed again.

TABLE OF CONTENTS

Part Three
Tea With Terrorists

Part Four
Reflections

Duke with Governor Mike Huckabee

FOREWORD

Duke Westover is one of those people you meet that you never forget. His story is a fascinating journey filled with incredible experiences at nearly every turn in the road. His life is filled with challenges, obstacles, failures and blessings. From his humble beginning and difficult childhood in Texas, he traces the hand of God in his life at every step of his journey.

I was deeply moved as I read about him and Carlene raising their daughter Kim, who was born with Spina Bifida. Her story of courage, faith and determination is a challenge to all of us who face life's greatest obstacles. Their devotion as parents is an example for every parent who must trust God to do the impossible in their lives.

My heart was also moved as I read the amazing story of Duke's commitment to Dr. Jerry Falwell, for whom he worked as executive assistant for more than 30 years. Duke's close personal relationship with Jerry allowed him to see this great servant of God up close and personal as they worked and traveled together all over the world. He not only shares the story of Dr. Falwell founding the Thomas Road Baptist Church, Liberty University and the Moral Majority, he also reveals incredible stories about Dr. Falwell that have never been in print before – the flying pie, the beignet disaster, the wild ride in the pickup truck and the night Jerry's pants fell down! You will laugh and cry as Duke takes you along on their amazing journey.

The most captivating story in the book is Duke's experience of interviewing Muslim terrorists in Bethlehem. Traveling with Craig Winn, who was doing research for a book of his own, Duke met with representatives of Hamas, Hezbollah, Al Fatah, Al Qaeda and Islamic Jihad. The insights he gained from their conversations provide a window into the mind and soul of Islamic extremists. Sit with him. Listen, as he has Tea with Terrorists. Their comments will help you better understand the challenges we face in the Middle East today.

Every life is a unique gift of God and Duke's life has been especially blessed. He has written these memoirs of his journey to encourage fellow travelers on the road of life. Martin Luther once said, "We are not yet what we shall be but we are growing toward it, the process is not yet finished but it is going on, this is not the end but it is the road." Life is such a road. It is never all joy and no sadness. It is never success without failure or gain without pain. No matter who travels life's path there will be obstacles to face and pitfalls to avoid. Problems will have to be faced and decisions will have to be made. But in the process, lessons will be learned and new growth will be attained. As you read this amazing book, let your soul be blessed and your heart be challenged.

Life is a pilgrimage. It is a process of growth. There are no shortcuts to success. You can only get there by walking the rough road of life. Never content with the temporal, we press on to the eternal. Every step of faith takes us further on the journey. And sometimes God blesses us with the ride of a lifetime. This is the story of just such a ride. Read it. Enjoy it. Experience it for yourself. For what God has done for Duke, He can do for you.

—Mike Huckabee

The Author

The world has yet to see what God will do with ....the man who is fully consecrated to Him."
Dwight L. Moody

I worked with that man for more than 38 years. His name was Jerry Falwell.

PROLOGUE

I recently saw a quote that reminded me of Jerry Falwell and the way he lived life.

"Life is not a journey to Heaven with the intention of arriving safely in a pretty and well-preserved body, but rather to skid broadside, thoroughly use up, totally worn out, and loudly proclaiming WOW! WHAT A RIDE!"

In May of 2009, my wife Carlene and I were invited to a function in Washington, D.C., to celebrate the 61st anniversary of the founding of the nation of Israel. There were many people there from both Israel and the United States in business and politics. I knew many of them from my days of traveling with Jerry Falwell and others because DuCar International Tours, a wholesale tour operation that Carlene and I founded in 1981, is a major force in tourism in Israel.

The host of the program that night was Rabbi Benny Elon, a former cabinet member in the Ariel Sharon government and a personal friend for many years. Benny was introducing me to some of the distinguished guests. One was Mike Pence, a U.S. Congressman from Indiana. He said, "Mike, I want you to meet Duke Westover. He was Jerry Falwell's right hand and traveled with him everywhere." The congressman took my hand and said, "Wow, what a ride." I said, "Congressman, if I ever write a book, you may have just named it."

FUNERAL PRAYER
May 22, 2007

Father, we are humbled to be in your presence today. We know, Father, that you never promised us tomorrow—but you did promise us eternity.

Father, we want to thank you for dreams.

- Without dreams, Father, there would not be a Thomas Road Baptist Church.

- Without dreams, Father, there would not be an Old-Time Gospel Hour Television Network and 3.5 million people who have told us that they came to faith in Christ as a result.

- Without dreams, there would not be an Elim Home for Alcoholics or the Liberty Godparent Home.

- There would not be a Liberty University and 120,000 alumni.

Father, we want to thank you for the dreamer.

- A man who dared to believe he could change a nation and a culture and maybe even a world.

- A man who dared to believe that lives could be changed and families could be put back together.

- A dreamer who could walk with kings and still be the pastor of a small-town church.

Father, although we are here to celebrate the home going of our giant of a leader, we also weep because we will miss him. We lost a brother, a father, a grandfather, a best friend and above all a husband and lover.

Today, Macel has a giant unimaginable hole in her heart and only a supernatural touch from You will begin to ease the pain.

But Father, these are truly the Days of Elijah. The mantle of leadership has fallen on two very qualified men chosen and trained by You just for this day.

Help us now, Father, to carry on the work. Help us rise to the challenge.

Help us be Your instruments to fulfill and finish the work begun by Jerry so that one day, when we meet him in glory, he will echo the words of our Heavenly Father: "Well done."

Father, hold us now in Your hand as we hold the entire Falwell family up in prayer.

This we pray in the name of our Savior, Jesus Christ. Amen.

I was humbled and honored that the Falwell family asked me to participate in the memorial service by opening in prayer. By nature, I am an emotional person and this was the toughest thing I had ever been asked to do. God alone got me through it.

One week earlier, Tuesday, May 15, 2007 at 12:40 p.m., Jerry Falwell was pronounced dead. He was my pastor, my mentor, my boss, my traveling companion and most of all, my best friend. After I prayed, I sat on the platform of Thomas Road Baptist Church looking at thousands of people who felt almost as badly as I did. Ron Godwin, Jim Moon, George Rogers, Franklin Graham and Jerry Vines each eulogized the man who had made such an incredible impact on their lives. Elmer Towns and Harold Wilmington each read from the Scriptures. Tim Goeglein read a moving message from President George W. Bush.

We were all comforted by songs from Charles Billingsley and Kendra Cook. Then, in a private ceremony, a few of us said our personal goodbyes as he was buried on Liberty Mountain. I had worked with Jerry for more than 38 years.

In retrospect, I think of another funeral.

-2-

FOOTPRINTS

Kathy Rusk was Dr. Jerry Falwell's administrative assistant and was the first contact when someone wanted him to speak at an event, perform a wedding, or conduct a funeral. When a request came, Kathy and I would go over the request to see if it fit into his already overbooked schedule. Occasionally a request would come for which we needed special guidance from Jerry.

As the pastor of Thomas Road Baptist Church, Jerry would almost always rearrange his schedule to accommodate funerals and weddings for members of the church. I remember once, when he performed three weddings and conducted four funerals on the same Saturday.

One day, Kathy received a call from a member of the church asking about Dr. Falwell's availability to conduct the funeral of her brother, who had died while visiting her in Lynchburg. When I went to Jerry with this request, he said to rearrange the schedule and make it fit.

I called the lady to let her know of the decision and to ask her some specifics about her brother. I asked if he had any family. She said their parents had died many years earlier, there were no other siblings, and her brother had never married. I asked her if her brother was a Christian— if he ever made a profession of faith in Christ. She answered, "Not to my knowledge."

I asked where her brother worked. She said that he was in between jobs. When I asked if he had ever received any recognition or awards that Dr. Falwell could mention, she thought for a few minutes and said, "Once he told me that he had been elected as assistant treasurer of his motorcycle club."

To help her out financially, the funeral service was held in the chapel at Thomas Road Baptist Church. We had to get staff members of the church to act as pallbearers, because only four people attended the service.

As we were driving to the cemetery, Jerry looked at me and said, "It would be terrible for a person to come to the end and all that can be said about him at his funeral is that 'once he had been the assistant treasurer of a motorcycle club'—God help me to leave more footprints than that."

I have never forgotten that statement and on May 15, 2007, Jerry Falwell left more footprints than any person I have ever met or heard about.

When it became evident that Jerry was having some health issues, everywhere we traveled, people would ask me privately, "Duke, who is going to take Jerry's place if something happens to him?" I would always answer in two parts. First, I would ask, "Whose place did Jerry take? The answer is no one. God raised up Jerry at a specific time, gave him a dream to change the world in his lifetime, and God will raise up someone else to continue the dream."

I would then say, "That person may or may not be a Falwell. The reason I say that is, through Thomas Road Baptist Church, the Old-Time Gospel Hour, Liberty Christian Academy, and Liberty University, Jerry has transferred that dream to hundreds of thousands of Jerry Falwells around the world."

In God's wisdom, the leadership mantel was passed to his two sons, Jerry Jr., who is Chancellor and President of Liberty University and Jonathan, who pastors Thomas Road Baptist Church. That transition has been seamless and the dream continues. These two young men will create their own footprints.

PART 1

MY STORY

-3-

MY JOURNEY

I want to tell you a story. This story is a cross between a bad novel and a soap opera. Some of the things you will read will be difficult to believe. I assure you that this is a true story.

The story covers more than 110 years and many characters. You almost need a program to keep up with the players.

When I first told Jerry Falwell this story, he said that everyone should hear it but that I should not tell it publicly until after my mother's death. You will understand why as you read further. Not long after my mother's death, he asked me to tell this story to Thomas Road on a Sunday night. He promoted it in the newspaper and on television and at the morning service. The building was almost full as people heard the story for the first time.

This story begins in the late 1890s in rural Alabama. It was only about 30 years after the devastating and demoralizing Civil War and Alabama was said to closely resemble a third-world country. Industry was decimated and all that was left of an economy was rooted in agriculture. The land owners had to rely on share croppers instead of slaves to plant and harvest their crops. There was no transportation to get the crops to the marketplace, so the crops were used mainly to feed the families who owned the land and the share croppers who worked the land.

In the midst of this poverty and misery, Frankie Lee McCarty was born. She was the youngest of three girls.

In this environment, giving birth to boys, who could eventually work in the fields, was reason for celebration. Girls, on the other hand, were more of a liability. And the McCartys had three of them.

At the ripe old age of 13, Frankie was married off to Bogan McQuege. The newlyweds moved in with Bogan's bachelor brother who was renting a farm house, a barn, and a few acres of farm land outside of Andalusia, Alabama. Frankie began having babies right away. By the time she was 20 years old, she had 6 children. None of them were twins.

Bogan worked in town and Frankie stayed home with the kids. One day, Bogan came home unexpectedly and found Frankie in bed with his brother. The fight with his brother began in the house with angry words and throwing of lamps, pots, pans, dishes, and anything that was not nailed down. It continued on the porch and then into the backyard and finally ended in the barn more than an hour later.

In the barn, Bogan's brother reached for his double barrel shotgun and Bogan reached for a trace chain that was hanging on a post. Bogan swung the chain just as his brother fired the first shot. A pellet from that shot lodged in Bogan's left eye. His brother was knocked to the ground by the force of the chain. From a sitting position, he fired the other barrel, severing Bogan's right leg just below the knee. Bogan, using his one good leg, raised himself up with his back against the post and struck his brother with a roundhouse blow with the chain that rendered him unconscious. Bogan struck his brother several more times with the chain until he was certain that he was dead.

Bogan crawled to his mule and, with great effort, difficulty, and determination, got on the animal's back. As he rode out of the barn door and through the backyard, he could see his 20-year-old wife and his 6 kids (the youngest of which was 5 months old) standing on the porch watching in horror. He was not seen again by Frankie or any of his kids for decades.

Except for her 6 kids, Frankie was all alone. She had no way to support herself. Her infidelity had led to the death of her brother-in-law and the maiming of her husband who had not been seen since he killed his brother. She was not welcome in the community.

Her tragedy did not end that day. The next 12 months saw her standing over the gravesites of three of her six children. One died of scarlet fever, another drowned, and the third burned to death as her nightgown caught fire when an ember popped from the fireplace. She had three children left—all boys.

-4-

MOBILE, ALABAMA

Just after dawn one morning, Frankie found herself and her three children on the porch of an orphanage in Mobile, Alabama. Basil, at five years, was the oldest. Glyn was three and Morgan, the baby, was 18 months.

She placed Morgan in a basket and pinned a note to Basil's shirt. She rang the door bell and quickly walked away. The note read, "I love my babies, but I can no longer take care of them."

I don't know how long the boys were in the orphanage.

It's possible that they were moved to another facility in Mobile.

One day, a group of law enforcement officers came to the orphanage. They were in the city for the Southern Sheriff's Convention and FBI training. The convention and training lasted for 3 weeks. While they were there, the officers visited the local hospitals, homes for the elderly, and orphanages to see how they measured up to the ones in their home towns and counties.

One Sheriff from Mississippi visited the orphanage of the three boys and struck up a friendship. He made it a point to see them every day for three weeks. Just before he returned home, he told the boys that he was engaged to be married and in a few weeks he was going to come back and adopt all three of them.

The boys were thrilled. They packed up their meager belongings in paper bags and everyday they sat at the front window and watched the driveway. Then one afternoon as they sat with hope and eagerness, they saw a police car drive up and the Sheriff and his new bride begin to walk up the sidewalk toward the porch. As the two younger boys began to shout for joy, Basil's eyes grew in amazement and he said, "That's Sheriff Westover, and he's with our mama."

That's right. Without knowing it, he had married their mother (I told you this was like a soap opera).

The logical question to ask is, did she know that he was going to adopt children? Did she tell him in advance that she had children? I don't know the answer. I do know that he did not know these were her children until that moment. I also know that the boys did not care one way or the other. That day they got their mother back, they got a father, and before long, they acquired a new name. They were no longer the McQuege kids—now they were Westovers. They were the sons of the Sheriff. If this was a fairy tale, the next line would be, *"And they lived happily ever after."*

As it turned out, ever after only lasted a few short years, because, while visiting her mother in Houston, Texas, Frankie met a man she would rather live with than her husband. His name was Eugene. She moved in with Eugene and sent for her boys. The boys boarded a train in Jackson, Mississippi, in route to a new adventure. Basil was 13, Glyn was 11, and Morgan was 9.

Two years later, Glyn ran away from home. Although he was only 13, he looked older. He forged his mother's signature on a letter that stated he was 17 and it gave her permission for him to join the Army.

-5-

MARRIAGE

Just before he was discharged from the Army at age 18, Glyn met Eva Griffee. She was 16 years old. Her mother had died when Eva was 10 and she was then living with her married sister and her husband.

Glyn and Eva married just after she turned 17. Nine months later, almost to the day, Eva gave birth to a baby boy. They named him William Eugene (after his great grandfather and one of his grandmother's husbands/lovers). William was immediately given the nickname Duke. So, I entered this convoluted mess on January 14, 1936.

Conventional wisdom would tell you that at some

point, a small grain of normalcy would creep into a family lineage. I assure you that this was not the case. The ingrained family pattern of deceit and infidelity continued. The only change was the addition of alcohol. My parents were constantly at war with each other over jealousy, infidelity, and alcohol. They were not alcoholics—the word was not fashionable yet. They were just plain drunks. They both drank heavily. Most of the time, they drank together, but my dad often drank with friends.

I remember my father coming home drunk one night. He plopped down on the bed and said, "Boy, take off my shoes."

We were living in a one room apartment above a two car garage. The kitchen, bedroom, dining, and living room were all the same room. We had a bathroom, but the toilet was a path in the backyard. I slept on an Army cot.

When my dad told me to take off his shoes, my mother went to the kitchen area and got a large iron skillet. She said, "Don't you come home drunk and tell my boy to take off your shoes." My dad started to get to his feet just as she, using both hands on the skillet, swung it like a baseball bat and hit him in the chest.

The blow knocked him completely over the bed where he landed on the floor against the wall. He remained there the rest of the night. To describe their relationship as stormy would be like describing the Grand Canyon as a pothole.

It all came crashing down when I was six years old standing in a courtroom, looking up at a judge sitting behind the biggest desk I had ever seen. I came to the courtroom with my grandmother. I had no idea why I

Miss E, Skipper and Duke, 1941

was there. When I walked in, I saw my mother standing to my right with her lawyer and my father on my left with his lawyer.

The judge acknowledged my presence and then looked back and forth to my parents and their lawyers and said, "Isn't anybody going to petition the court for custody?" No one spoke. Neither of my parents would look at me. They just stared at the judge. Finally, he looked down at me and said, "Son, your mother and dad don't want to live together anymore. I have given them what we call a divorce. The only issue that has not been settled is who you are going to live with. This is the only divorce case that I have seen where neither party petitioned for custody. So, I guess it falls to me to make that choice for them." He went on to say, "I don't know them very well and I don't know you at all, but I can see you're a big boy and I am going to let you make that decision. If you want to live with your mother, walk to her. If you want to live with your father, walk to him."

I was smarter than the average six-year-old. I didn't move. I sat down in the middle of the floor and wept. I wasn't as big as he thought I was. After a while, the judge decided that I would go and live with my grandmother, Frankie, who was married to her fourth of five husbands. It wasn't all that bad. She really loved me.

-6-

KIDNAPPED

My father remarried right away and then filed for divorce less than a year later. My mother moved to Port Arthur, Texas, about 100 miles from me and my grandmother. While I was living with my grandmother, her husband, Eugene Roberts, had a massive heart attack and died. Dad Roberts really was a good man. He loved me just like my grandmother did and showed it openly.

Eighty eight days after her fourth husband died, Frankie married Theo Dummer. It was said that she did not marry for love—she just loved to marry.

I was in the second grade at Elliott Elementary School in Houston, Texas. One afternoon at recess, my mother met me on the playground and kidnapped me. We went to live with my aunt in Port Arthur. I was enrolled in school there, and about a month later, my dad found me at recess and kidnapped me back. Again I was with my grandmother. I always knew she loved me.

Although their divorce had been finalized for quite a while, the issue of my custody was still in question. After the kidnappings, their lawyers got involved again. During a meeting one day, both attorneys expressed frustration with this case. They said, "We can file suits and go to court forever, but there are only two people who can solve this issue—the mother and father." With that in mind, the attorneys tricked my mother and father into meeting. The attorneys locked them in a conference room and said, "We will not let you out until someone says, 'I want Duke to live with me.'"

They remained in the conference room for four hours before they knocked on the door and said, "We have reached a decision." The attorneys said, "It's about time. What is the decision?" My dad said, "We've decided to get married again."

Once again, the next line should be "*and they lived happily ever after.*"

Unfortunately, this is not a fairy tale. Nothing really changed. The culture of infidelity, alcohol, and deceit was ingrained. Over the next five years, they filed for divorce twice and were separated innumerable times. Once, my mother left in a huff and was gone for three months.

I must pause here for a moment to explain the relationship between my parents and me. It's easy to read this narrative and come to the conclusion that I was not loved by my parents. On this subject, let me be perfectly clear. I have never one time in my life felt unloved. It was just different.

Almost from the day I took my first step at nine months, we were three adults living in the same house. One of us was just a lot shorter than the other two. It was not that I was unloved as a child. The fact is, I never was a child.

My father's name was Douglas Glyn. As a young man,

he acquired the nickname Skipper. From that day forward, no one called him by anything but Skipper, because no one knew his real name.

My mother's name was Eva. Because she always signed her name E. Westover, someone started calling her, Miss E. Before long, no one knew what her real name was. I told you that my name is William Eugene, and as a baby my dad gave me the nickname Duke.

I never called my parents mother and dad—they were always Skipper and Miss E. I cannot remember a time that I was ever kissed by my father. Even as a four year old, we always shook hands. My mother and I hugged but rarely kissed. This had nothing to do with respect, love, or honor; we were just three adults living in the same house.

To everyone, we were the Westovers, Skipper, Miss E, and Duke. My grandmother called me Billy Gene.

To give you a sense of not being a child, one day when I was eight years old, my dad, who (along with my mother) was a two-pack-a-day smoker, asked me, "Do you think you will smoke when you grow up?" I said, "I guess so." "Well, do you want to start now?" I shook my head yes, so he pulled out a half empty pack of Camels and gave me one. He said, "Keep the pack," and he struck a match to light it.

For the rest of the day, every time I thought about it, I lit up another cigarette. It took me until the next afternoon to finish the pack. When I smoked the last one, I said to myself, "What's so great about smoking?" From that day forward, I never smoked another cigarette. You may ask, was he trying to teach me a lesson? I have no idea. It never came up again.

In addition, liquor and beer was always in the cabinet

or the refrigerator and was always available to me if I wanted it. After tasting them, I decided that was something for which I would have to acquire a taste. So I wondered, why bother? I also saw how it affected my parents and I wanted nothing to do with it.

I was given responsibility very early. When I was 10, my dad went into the sheet metal business. It was a tough struggle without resources, but he was a great salesman and a good businessman. He needed a vehicle and a trailer to carry sheet metal to a job site, so he bought a war surplus jeep. Before long, he acquired a pickup truck and for my 12th birthday, he gave me the jeep. That's right; I had my own car when I was 12. The day I was 14, I got my driver's license and was given a 1948 green Studebaker convertible. I was in the eighth grade and was the only kid who drove his car to school.

The summer that I was 15, Bob Knox (my best friend) and I took a two week vacation to Florida and Tennessee by ourselves. That fall, I decided that I wanted to go to a military school in Kerrville, Texas. The tuition, room, and board was $1,500. My family did not have the money, so I sold my car for $1,200 and my dad gave me the rest.

I grew up fast.

-7-

WAR YEARS

During World War II, my father worked in maintenance and construction on military bases, defense facilities and ship building yards in 11 different states. For a long time, when people would ask me where I was raised,

I would respond, "In the back seat of a 1941 Oldsmobile, with a dog, a cat, a bird, and a rabbit." Most of the time, the animals got along reasonably well. However, Lady, our Boston terrier, tolerated cats, but did not like them.

One morning, just as I left for school, my mother found Snow Ball, the cat, dead with a broken neck. She thought that I would be upset, so she went to the pound and got another cat the same color (white) and size as Snow Ball and hoped I would not know the difference. However, by the time I got home from school, that cat was dead, too. I told you Lady was sick of having a cat around. For some reason, she liked the rabbit.

After the war ended in 1945, my father went into the sheet metal and air conditioning business. He started on a shoestring with little money and used equipment. The timing and place for a venture like that was good. The heat and humidity in Houston ,Texas, is legendary and the public drive to air-condition everything was paramount. After about three years business was good enough for us to build a small house of our own.

Not long after we moved into our new home, a couple moved into the house next to us: Mr. and Mrs. Pavlock. They were very nice people and they were Christians. They were the worst possible kind of Christians that you could have living next door; they were witnessing Christians. Every time they would see us in the yard or see us drive into our garage, they would say, "You all need to go to church with us. We have the best preacher you have ever heard. The music is great and there are a lot of young people and especially girls, Duke's age." That part started to get to me, because I had healthy hormones as a 13-year-old.

Each time they would corner us, we would say, "one of these days we'll go to church with you." We never had any intentions of going to church with them.

It was March of 1950, two months after my 14th birthday. One Sunday afternoon, my father was reading the newspaper and saw the advertisement of a movie that he had wanted to see. He and my mother drove to the theatre. When they arrived, they were told the movie would not start for another 45 minutes. Not wanting to enter the theatre too soon, they decided to kill some time. They saw a drug store a couple blocks away that had a soda fountain. They decided to go there and get a malted milk while they waited for the movie to begin.

When they drove up to the drug store, they saw that it was next door to a church. There were no parking spaces in front of the drug store and no parking places in front of the church. They had to park on the other side of the church and walk back to the drug store. As they walked in front of the church, my dad stopped and looked up toward the sign and said to my mother, "Berean Baptist Church; isn't that where the Pavlocks go to church?" Before my mother could answer, a lady came up behind them, put her arms around each of them and said, "It sure is and we are glad to have you visiting us tonight." With that she ushered them right through the front door and into the church sanctuary just as the Sunday evening service was beginning. They enjoyed the service and loved the fact that people made them welcome. They went back the next Sunday morning and I went with them Sunday night.

I was fascinated by the friendliness of everyone that I met. I looked around at the young people and especially the pretty girls. As the service began, the choir took its place. Immediately I noticed the girl on the top row, second from the end. She had dark hair, green eyes, and a smile that would melt the chrome off of a 1949 Cadillac.

I leaned over to my mother and asked, "Who is that?" She said, "I don't know her name, but the man right in front of you is her father. This morning, I saw him giving her some money."

I leaned over and tapped her father on the shoulder (as you can tell, I was shy) and asked, "Sir, what is your daughter's name?" He turned his head a little and said, "Carlene." I looked at her again and tapped him again and asked, "Carlene, what?"

He is the only person I have ever seen who could sit facing forward and not rotate his shoulders at all and turn his head all the way around and look me in the eye. He said, "Wilson." After services that night, I met Carlene Wilson. I have never been the same. Two nights later, Berean had church-wide visitation and the Wilson family got the Westover family's visitors card and came to visit us.

Carlene was an only child and I was an only child. That night, our parents met for the first time and instantly became best friends. From that night forward, it was just understood that Carlene and I would grow up and get married. Sure enough, we did.

The next Sunday, the Westover family walked down the center aisle and joined the Berean Baptist Church in Houston. The last church we had attended was a Baptist church; therefore we could join by letter. None of us were saved at the time.

Change in our family culture did not come easily. However, it did come. My mother came to faith first and my father was saved later.

At last, I became a part of a family that had spiritual values and lived in a morally-based world—unfortunately; it was not the family in which I was born.

-8-

THE WILSONS

You've had a glimpse of the chaotic family culture in which I was raised; now I want to tell you about a family that is 180 degrees from that. Carlene grew up in a Christian Ozzie and Harriett environment.

Carl Wilson, her dad, worked at the same job for 42 years. He was a machinist at Hughes Tool Company in Houston. The company was owned by Howard Hughes and was one of the best run companies in the nation. They began in 1909 making roller cutting drill bits for the oil industry. Those bits revolutionized the oil drilling industry. During the war years, Hughes Tool was refitted to manufacture parts for war planes.

Every morning, Carl would leave home at 6:15 and walk the six blocks from his home to the plant. Promptly at 3:00 in the afternoon, his wife, Grayce, would drive to the gate and pick him up. Dinner would be on the table when they arrived home.

Carl and Grayce were both from a farming community near Huntsville, Texas. Carl's grandfather was the pastor of a small country church. Grayce's father had also given land to build a church building (not the same church). They both came to faith in Christ at an early age and it was in that environment that they grew up, met, and married.

They married in 1931 and settled in Houston. When they decided to build a house of their own, Carl's brothers and other friends helped and the house was finished just before Carlene was born in 1936. She lived in that same house until she and I married in 1954. That was quite a contrast from my upbringing; I lived in 11 different states before I was 10 years old.

The whole Wilson family was active in the Berean Baptist Church. If fact, Carl and Grayce were the Sunday school superintendents of the 9 to 12 year olds until Grayce died in 1974. Carlene began playing the piano and organ at the church when she was 15. These were people who took the Bible admonition literally and did not forsake the assembling together of the church.

Carl Wilson was the poster boy of spiritual giants; he was the godliest man I ever knew. When God wrote the 31st chapter of Proverbs, He must have had Carlene's mother in mind.

The satanic syndrome of my heritage and lineage was shattered because of them. Grayce and Carl Wilson were now my spiritual mentors and role models.

-9-

CHURCH YEARS

Although my parents were saved (and I have no doubt that they were), Satan was alive and well and had a remaining stranglehold on my dad and mother. At times they tried hard. But, in the end, it was a losing effort for both of them—especially for my dad. He was killed in a private plane crash in 1962. God called him home early.

When my parents and Carlene's parents met and became best friends, it was just understood that Carlene and I would someday marry. And we did, on October 23, 1954. Carlene was the church pianist and I sang in the choir and led the music in various classes. We were the church sweethearts. There were more than 750 people who attended our wedding.

At the time, I was working as a sheet metal worker on the construction of a high-rise building in downtown Houston. I was also in the U.S. Navy Reserve. Less than two months after we married, I received the notice that I had been activated. One week after my 19th birthday, I was in the U.S. Navy and on my way to Charleston, South Carolina.

I was permanently stationed at Chase Naval Auxiliary Air station in Beeville, Texas. I was just 180 miles from Houston for my entire two-year commitment. I cannot count the number of times I hitchhiked to and from Beeville.

My job in the Navy began with Flight Operations in the control tower. Later, I was appointed as aide to the Chief Operations Officer. I maintained his office and schedule and traveled with him occasionally.

With that job came a Class A liberty pass, which meant that I never had to stand watch and had every weekend off. Therefore, virtually every weekend, I went home. The last 18 months that I was in Beeville, I worked as the evening disc jockey and did the news on a local radio station. That set the stage for working as one of the earliest Gospel disc jockeys in the nation in Houston in the 1960s.

-10-

KIM

Eleven months after I was called to active duty, our only child was born. We named her Taryn Kim. I was at the hospital the night Kim was born. She was the most beautiful baby I had ever seen. She was small, only 15 ½ inches long and 5 lbs. 15 ounces. From outward appearances she looked perfect.

When Carlene was sufficiently awake, the doctor came in to give us the news about our beautiful daughter. He said she was born with Spina Bifida; a defect in the spinal column where the spinal cord is exposed. If left untreated, the spinal cord would be subjected to infections and she would probably not live for more than six months.

He said, however, that there was a new procedure he could recommend that would close the opening in her back and reduce the chances for infection. With that operation, she would probably live about 18 years. That was the life expectancy of a child with her condition. Well, the Lord worked a miracle in Kim. On November 3, 2009, she turned 54 years old. The point of this story comes down to one word: Carlene.

I want to paint a word picture here for a moment. When the doctor told us about Kim's condition and the options, Carlene and I had been married a little more than a year. I would be in the military for another 14 months and was making a grand total of $199 per month. We had no insurance. The hospital bill was going to be astronomical. Carlene knew that she would be the caregiver of a handicapped child no matter how long the child lived.

Without any hesitation or consultation with family, Carlene looked at me and said I believe we should have the operation. This is the decision of a very spiritually mature Christian; a spiritually mature Christian woman who had just turned 19 years old.

As soon as she was physically able, she got a job to help pay off the debt. Her mother helped with Kim during the day, but at night she was both mother and dad, because I was still in the Navy. After my discharge, I was working, Carlene was working, and I was going to college. We were the youth directors of our church and Carlene was the church pianist.

Yes, we were busy. We were very busy, but Kim was with us every minute. Carlene became an expert at what would later be known as multi-tasking. She never complained. She never thought she had a burden.

When Kim was old enough for school, she was home schooled. Carlene was her teacher. She was and is the closest thing to Super Woman that I have ever known. She is my best friend, my wife, my lover, my companion, the mother of my child, my business partner, my cheer leader, and my critic.

How do you tell a woman like that that you love her? I will tell you how I tell her. Every morning, the first thing I say is, "Good morning, I love you." The last thing I say at night is, "Good night, I love you. " Every time I leave home, I say, "Goodbye, I love you." At the end of a phone call, I say, "Goodbye, I love you."

Today, we have been married 55 years. The odds tell us that I will likely die before she does. If so, I want her to remember that the last words she heard me say were, "I love you."

Would you like to know the neatest thing about all of that? She loves me, too. She really does. How can you top that? I have a wife who loves me, I have a wonderful daughter who loves me, I have friends who love me, I have a God who loves me, and I have a Savior who loved me enough to die for me. It doesn't get any better than that.

There is so much more to this story that I promise to tell you in another chapter. I told you my mother was saved first and my father's salvation came later. Now, I must tell you about my salvation experience; how I came to faith in Christ.

I was discharged from the Navy 10 days after my 21st birthday. I had a wife and a 15-month-old daughter. Carlene was working to help pay off a huge medical debt and to send me to college. I was discharged from the Navy, started a job and started college, all on the same day.

Three weeks later, February 10, 1957, in the Sunday evening service at the Berean Baptist Church, the pastor made a statement that got my attention. He said, "If you were the only person on earth—Jesus would still have had to leave His place in the throne room of heaven and come to earth and die. He volunteered to die for sinners. If you are a sinner—and you are—He would have had to die because you sinned. He is asking to be your personal savior.

Here is God's promise: if you will accept Jesus as your personal Savior, He, God, will save you. Therefore, if you do accept Jesus, God is obligated to save you. He is God, and He cannot lie."

He continued, "Was there a time in your life that you knew you were lost and there was nothing you could do about it?" He further said, "It is impossible to accept Jesus as Savior until you know you are lost and need a Savior." That made sense to me.

That moment I believed and trusted God's promise that He would save me when I accepted Jesus as my personal Savior.

I wish I could tell you that at that moment lightning flashed across the sky, cannons boomed, and angels were singing. I wish I could say that at that moment I felt a very heavy burden of guilt lifted from my shoulders. That's how Hollywood would have portrayed this event. However, nothing like that happened. I simply passed from head knowledge of Jesus to heart knowledge of Jesus. It was an intellectual decision. There was no emotion what so ever.

-11-

TRAGEDY

I was now 21 years old, attending college at night, working as a sheet metal apprentice during the day. Carlene was working at Humble Oil Company and Carlene's mother was taking care of Kim.

We were very involved in our church. Carlene was church pianist, I sang in the choir and led worship in various Sunday school classes, and was occasionally asked to lead our choir.

I was working for my father as a sheet metal worker and designing and installing air conditioning systems. On the weekends, I was a gospel disc jockey on three different radio stations.

In every man's life, there are a number of defining

moments. September 6, 1962, was one of those moments for me. Carlene and I had gone to Sulfur, Louisiana, to a gospel music concert. We were originally going to fly. I had received my pilot's license about 18 months earlier and my father owned a Cessna 182 airplane.

When I checked the weather forecast, I noticed that, although the weather was going to be good, there was a chance of ground fog about the time that we would be returning. It was only a two and a half hour drive, so we decided to drive instead of flying.

My father, who was not a pilot, called Jimmy Rice, our choir director, and asked him if he wanted to go flying. Jimmy was a brand new pilot and was always looking for an opportunity to fly.

When Carlene and I returned home about 3:00 a.m., my mother called and said that Skipper and Jimmy were missing. We drove immediately to the airport. We discovered that they had radioed that they were on base leg and turning final about 10:00 p.m., and had not been heard from since.

As soon as the sun came up, I got in a plane to try to find the wreckage. I found it just about a mile from the small airport. They had obviously settled into the fog, become disoriented, and crashed behind a ranch house. No one was home at the time, so the wreckage was not discovered until morning. Skipper and Jimmy were both killed instantly.

Both funerals were conducted at the Berean Baptist Church the same day, four hours apart. There were more than 1,000 people at my father's service. The processional to the cemetery was more than a mile long.

For reasons that I will not discuss here, I am convinced

that God called my father home prematurely. I know in my heart that he was saved.

One week after the funeral, my mother met with my dad's partner to exercise the buy and sell agreement of their business. The partner was more than generous with my mother and paid her more than he was required under their agreement.

My father told me for years, speaking of the company, that someday it would all be mine. Well, his partner bought my mother out and promptly shut down the business.

Not only was it not all mine, but I was also unemployed.

For the next two and a half years I worked as a roofing and sheet metal contractor and a mechanical engineer for an air conditioning company.

In 1965, I decided that I wanted to get into the church building business. I had heard of a company in Cleburne, Texas, that built churches. I drove to Cleburne, met the owner, and he hired me that day.

That began the ride of a lifetime. As of today, I have been involved in the construction of more than 200 church buildings in 31 states.

-12-

THE OTHER WOMAN IN MY LIFE

Everyone who has a child or grandchild believes that their boy or girl is the most beautiful and the smartest kid on earth. They also believe that they say the cutest things.

I am reminded of a man who was trapped on a plane next to a very talkative lady and had to endure a litany of stories and tales about one grandchild after another. Finally she asked, "Have I shown you pictures of my grandchildren?"

"No," he answered, "and really do appreciate it."

Having said that, I want to tell you what happened one night when my daughter, Kim, was three years old.

We were living in Houston, Texas, in an apartment built over a three car garage. The way that the apartment was arranged, you had to go through the kitchen to get to any room in the house. From the living room to our bedroom, you had to go through the kitchen. From our bedroom to Kim's bedroom, you had to go through the kitchen.

Kim, as I told you earlier, was born with Spina-Bifida and was paralyzed from her waist down. She learned to get around by pulling herself along the floor with her arms and upper body. She was always a happy child and never felt sorry for herself.

I had been out of the Navy for about one year. I was going to college and working as a sheet metal worker. Carlene and I were youth leaders at our church, and Carlene was the church pianist. To say the least, we were busy.

One Wednesday night after prayer meeting and choir practice, Carlene and I were exhausted and wanted to go to bed early. Kim decided she was not as tired as we were so she was not ready to go to bed.

We put her in her bed and knelt beside her bed in prayer. As we arose, we kissed her good night and started to turn off her light. She stopped me and asked if she could have a glass of water. I got her the water then kissed her again, turned out the light and started to go to bed. She asked if we could leave the light on a little while longer. I said "No, go to sleep." She said, "Well, I'm not sleepy." I told her, "Well, I don't care if you are sleepy or not; I am not leaving the light on."

I had been in the bed only a little while when I heard a soft voice saying, "Daddy, would you bring me a glass of water?" I said, "Kim, I just gave you some water. Now go to sleep."

"Daddy, I sure am thirsty. Please bring me some water." I said, "Kim, I am tired of this fooling around. Now go to sleep." She said, "Please daddy, I'm thirsty."

I said, "Kim, if you say another word, I am going to come in there and give you a spanking. Now go to sleep." Next she gave a deep sigh and said, "Ok daddy, but when you come through the kitchen, would you please bring me some water?"

Needless to say, she got her water.

Even though Kim was born, as some people would say, handicapped, she was always exceptional. I have told people that she thinks the rest of the world is handicapped because they do not have wheelchairs. She is bright, witty, and fun to be around. People who meet her for the first time have said, "After about 15 minutes, you forget that she is in a wheelchair." I am certain that at some time in her life, she has felt sorry for herself, but I can truthfully say, I have never seen it.

By the time Kim was ready for school, Carlene became a stay-at-home mom and became her teacher. That was during a period where handicapped children were not allowed in regular classes in the public schools.

In 1965, I went into the church building business and began traveling a lot. After a while we got a motor home and traveled as a family. I was building churches all over the country and was meeting with new prospects weekly.

I would schedule the meetings with new prospects in the evening when the members of the church building committee could meet. Carlene and Kim would perform school work during the day as we traveled to that destination. When we arrived at the church site, we would park our motor home and have dinner. Afterwards, I would dress for the meeting and Carlene and Kim would dress for bed. Later when I returned from the meeting, we would drive for a couple of hours and find a campground, hook-up, and spend the night. The next day we would do it all again.

It was a great experience. In one twelve month period, we drove our motor home to 47 of the contiguous states, missing only Michigan.

Kim graduated high school in 1974 from Kline High School in Houston, Texas, through their home school program. During the rehearsal for the graduation ceremonies, Kim was told by the lady in charge that a guy would be assigned to push her on to the football field first. The graduates would then march on to the field and take their places.

She further stated that all of the other graduates would march to the platform and received a handshake, congratulations, and a piece of paper.

After the completion of the ceremonies, all of the other graduates would march out. At that point, Kim would be taken to the gymnasium separately where all graduates would receive their actual diploma.

Kim said, "No ma'am." The lady seemed shocked. She looked as if she did not believe that anyone in a wheelchair could talk. Kim reached up to the lady's clip board and found her name. She pointed to it and said, "My name is here, in between these two people. I worked just as hard as the others did for this day, maybe harder, and I want to march across the platform just like the rest of the graduates and in the order my name should be called."

That night at the graduation ceremony, in the stands, there were about 20 people who came just to cheer her on. No other graduate had such a loud and rambunctious cheering section. Everyone was proud of Kim and her accomplishment.

Getting through 12 years of schooling was tough on her and Carlene. Carlene had just graduated from high school when Kim was born. Six years later, she became teacher for another 12 years. They were both exhausted. Carlene told her if she wanted to go to college, she was on her own.

It was 10 years before she decided to try college. She was 29 years old when she enrolled at Liberty University. The first classroom she was ever in was her first day in college.

She told me a few months earlier that she wanted to go to college. We were living in Atlanta at the time and I asked if she wanted to go to one of the local community colleges. "No," she said, "I want to go to Liberty University and live in the dorm." I took a deep breath and said, "Are you sure you can pull that off? I know you're independent, but that is a big step."

"No," she said, "I'm not sure, but I am sure of this: I want to try and I will give it all I've got." After spending the rest of the day talking through all of the ramifications and challenges, Carlene and I both said, "We will stand behind your decision."

She could not get everything done to get accepted for the fall semester so we took her to Lynchburg in January of 1985. When we arrived, there were 10 inches of snow on the ground and the temperature was 5 degrees. Kim has a terrible case of psoriasis. When the temperature drops below 75 degrees she is freezing.

When we arrived she looked at Carlene and said, "Well, God knew how much I wanted to come to Liberty. Now he is testing me to see if I will stay."

After she got through all of the registration process and moved into her dorm room, she was ready to go to class and we were ready to go home. I quickly kissed her goodbye and went to the car while Carlene said her good-byes. As we drove out of town we both began to openly weep. This was the first time in 29 years that Carlene and Kim had been separated for any length of time. Carlene was the first to speak. She said, "Why are we crying? This is the best thing that can happen to her. We have always thought that she is independent, but now she's going to prove it to us."

She had a few health problems that slowed her down, but she graduated in 1991 with a degree in broadcast journalism. When she graduated, she was the assistant news director of the campus radio station.

Not long after her graduation, we all moved to Lynchburg and she has been active, along with Carlene, in DuCar International, our wholesale tour company.

Kim loves to travel. She has been to the Middle East 13 times. Hawaii is her favorite destination. She and her best friend Connie McGarity have traveled there seven times. They take trips together in the states at least twice per year.

She once told me that although she wonders sometimes what it would have been like to get married and have children, she knows that she would have never been able to travel to every state (except Alaska) and many foreign countries had she done so. The other woman in my life may be in a wheelchair, but she is not handicapped.

-13-
FAMILY UPDATE

MY DAD'S BROTHERS

Morgan Westover, who was the youngest of the three boys, died in 1944 with Tuberculosis.

Basil Westover, the oldest, married and had three children. He became a drunk and a con man. He spent most of the final thirty years of his life in either a federal or state prison. He was finally released from the Texas Prison System when he was in his mid 70s. About six months after his release, he returned to the prison and asked if he could live in his cell and wash dishes for his keep. He said that his life had been so structured for so long, that he had no idea how to live in the outside world. He died about 3 years later.

MY GRANDFATHER

Bogan McQuege was my real grandfather. After he killed his brother in the fight over the infidelity of Frankie, he dropped out of sight and out of everybody's life for about three decades. One day in 1947, my dad got a call from his cousin, who was in the auto repair business in Pensacola, Florida, saying a man named Bogan McQuege came in to his shop and had brakes put on his car. Skipper got Bogan's address from the cousin and wrote Bogan a letter. Sure enough, the man was his father that he had not seen since he was three years old. After talking to him on the telephone, we drove from Houston to Pensacola for a long overdue reunion.

We learned that Bogan changed the spelling of his last name a number of times and moved around a great deal. He had married again and had 3 children by Tommie, his wife.

I am sure you are asking the same question that I asked. We know that a lot of the characters in this story were married a number of times, but you never hear of them getting a divorce. Simply, they did not get divorces. They just left town and started a new life in every respect.

As I said, Bogan and Tommie had three children. We maintained contact with them for about seven years. During that time, Rachael, the oldest, left her husband and three children and ran away with a man with whom she had been having an affair for about a year.

Bogan Jr. enlisted in the Army and within six months was given a dishonorable discharge. He stayed in trouble with the authorities for a long time after that.

The most interesting of the three was the youngest daughter, Christy. She married at the age of 16 and gave birth to two little girls within about 20 months. Her husband was in the U.S. Army and stationed not far from Pensacola. Just before the second child was born, he was transferred to Germany. A few months later, Christy met a traveling salesman from Texas, gave the two babies to her mother, Tommie, and went to Texas with her new friend.

Bogan, my grandfather, had no intention of living in the house with these babies. One day, he packed a suitcase, got on a train, and disappeared again.

Tommie had the two little girls, no husband, and no income. She contacted her son-in-law in Germany and he helped out with a little money and requested a hardship transfer back to the States.

In just a few weeks, he was transferred to Fort Hood, Texas. He sent Tommie enough money to ride the bus from Pensacola to Texas with the children. Tommie needed a place to live and he needed someone to care for the children during the day. It was the perfect answer to the problem.

It was not long, however, before he and his mother-in-law began sleeping together. They soon married, so she could receive spousal allotment pay from the Army.

Think about this, his mother-in-law is now his wife; his kids are now his grandkids and his ex-wife is his daughter. Not long after that, Christy and her salesman boyfriend came to visit, so she could see her children and her mother. They all stayed in the same house for a number of weeks.

Once again, it was like a soap opera.

In 2008, I was able to fill in some of the blanks on what happened to Bogan, my real grandfather, because I met Bogan's other grandson, Bogan III, via telephone.

After he left Pensacola, he lived in Maryland and worked as a deputy sheriff. I do not know the details but I was told that he shot and killed two people in two separate incidences while working there and was fired from the sheriff's department.

I was also told that, at the age of 79, he married an 18-year-old Native American girl. When she became pregnant with his child, a man from her tribe was berating her in public for marrying an old white man. Bogan took a garden rake and publicly beat the man to death.

That means that Bogan McQuege, my grandfather, killed 4 people in his lifetime and was never punished or prosecuted for any of these actions.

MY GRANDMOTHER (FRANKIE)

Frankie was the central character in the beginning of this book. There is so much more that could be written about her that it would fill another book. She was the one person that I could always count on to love me unconditionally.

She and her last husband both came to faith in Christ on the same night. She was in her 80's when she died.

MY FATHER

My father's complete name was Douglas Glyn Westover, but everyone knew him as Skipper.

He married my mother when he was 18 and she had just turned 17. Skipper had just been discharged from the Army. He had joined the Army, with forged papers, when he was 13.

Infidelity was a part of the inbred culture in which he was born. He and his two brothers were almost never in a structured family; therefore, there were never any rules to follow. The closest they came to a good male role model was Mr. Westover and he was not in the picture long enough to make an impression. His drinking and infidelity was the cause of constant conflict in his and my mother's marriage.

When our family became members of Berean Baptist Church, although my father was not yet saved, he did his best to change his life and fit into the spiritual structure created by adopting Carl Wilson (my future father-in-law) as his best friend.

My father and mother both stopped drinking entirely. The cupboards and the refrigerator were emptied of all alcohol and beer. Overnight, they acted as if they had been Christians for years. They changed their habits and their friends. Every time the doors of the church were open, they were there.

Frank Fort was our pastor. Carl Wilson, Frank Fort, and my dad were together constantly. In fact, three years in a row, the three families traveled together for vacations.

Later, my dad was appointed as one of the trustees of the church and then became treasurer. By all outward appearances, he was a candidate for the Christian of the Year award. My mother was the first to come to faith in Christ. She soon began teaching a Sunday school class.

A few years later, George Hodges, a pastor from Florida, was preaching a week of meetings at our church. The services were all well attended and the Holy Spirit seemed to be moving. There were almost no visible responses to the messages, until the last service on Sunday morning.

Dr. Hodges preached and gave the invitation. No one came forward. He turned the service back to Brother Fort, who said, "I believe that there are a number of people here who need to accept Jesus as personal savior and I want to give you one last chance." The music began again and my dad stepped out and came forward. He told the pastor, "I have known all along that I wasn't saved, but I continued acting like a Christian, hoping that doing good works would count for something. Now I know, good works is no substitute for accepting Christ."

When he walked down the aisle, it was like turning a bottle upside down and removing the cap. There were about 1,000 people in the service. Before the conclusion that day, 273 people came forward. About 80 came for salvation; more than 100 came for church membership and the rest for rededication. We saw genuine revival that day.

My father had a real born again experience. All outward signs pointed to a positive break in history and culture.

Although my father and mother loved each other in their own way, they never got to the place where they liked each other very much.

Before they were saved, my mother looked on my father's infidelities as just things that men do and if left alone, he would come home to her, which he always did. Now that they were both Christians, the ghosts of all those other women began to haunt her. She could not get it out of her mind, even though my dad had cleaned up his act and was now walking the straight and narrow path. Before long, my mother was so paranoid and jealous that she drove everyone around her crazy, especially my dad.

About three years after he came to faith, my father met a woman that, by his judgment, was everything my mother was not. Before long, things got out of hand and the old sinful nature manifested itself. He rented an apartment and set the new woman up in style.

At first, he was very discrete. My mother knew nothing of the woman, but her remembrance of ancient history drove him further and further away so he became less and less discrete.

I knew of the affair almost from the beginning. As he became more and more enamored, he was ready to leave my mother to marry the other woman. A scandal like that would have a devastating effect on our church.

Through a series of events, my mother found out about the affair and our pastor also found out.

My dad truly repented. He came before the church asking for prayer. The church people never knew the sordid details. He sent the other woman away to another part of Texas and was content to never see her again. He became a model husband and model church member and did everything in his power to rectify his transgressions.

My mother made his life a living hell. He tried everything. He begged for forgiveness. He gave her gifts. He played the perfect husband in every way. It was all sincere, but to no avail.

After about 18 months, he made contact with the other woman. He told her that he could no longer take the abuse and had decided to leave my mother and come live with her.

One week later, he was killed in a private plane crash.

MY MOTHER

When my father was killed, my mother enjoyed playing the part of the poor widow. Financially, she was left reasonably secure. She could have lived comfortably for the rest of her life if she was careful.

When my dad made the decision to leave, he told me

of his intentions. He also said that if anything ever happened to him, my mother would be broke within two years. He was right.

Within six months of my father's death, my mother was engaged to a man my age. She bought him a new Cadillac, a townhouse, and a diamond ring that was to be her wedding ring. A few days before the scheduled wedding, he took the car and the ring and moved another woman into the townhouse.

My mother turned on Carlene and me with a vengeance. She found out that we knew of my dad's affair and did not tell her. She accused me of having an affair with the daughter of the other woman. She treated Carlene and Kim shamefully. She began to drink again heavily.

Over the next few years, she was married three times to two different men. She and I finally made peace a few years later. It took Carlene a bit longer.

Later, we moved her to Atlanta to be close to us. When Carlene, Kim, and I moved to Lynchburg, she did not want to leave Atlanta. She died in 1998, at the age of 80.

Jerry Falwell speaking at a Pastor's Conference

PART 2

MY JOURNEY WITH
JERRY FALWELL

-14-

WOW! WHAT A RIDE

The real ride began in 1968 when I was constructing a building in Greensboro, North Carolina, for the Brightwood Baptist Church. During the construction of the building, the pastor, Ellis Adams, and I became great friends. One day in the fall of that year, Ellis said to me, "I just heard that Jerry Falwell is going to build a 3,000-seat sanctuary. You should go up there and talk to him." I asked, "Who is Jerry Falwell?" Ellis said, "Who is Jerry Falwell! Have you been living under a rock? He pastors the Thomas Road Baptist Church in Lynchburg, Virginia."

"It's the largest and fastest growing church in this part of the country," he said. "He has thousands of people attending Sunday school each week. Lynchburg is only about two hours up highway 29 from here."

I went in the pastor's office and called information in Lynchburg for the church's phone number. I called and asked to speak to Jerry Falwell. Jerry answered the phone on the first ring. I told him that I was in the business of building churches and that I was constructing a building for Ellis Adams in Greensboro. I told him that Ellis suggested that I call.

He told me that he had driven by Brightwood the week before and wondered who was doing the construction. After a few more minutes of conversation, he asked if I could come to Lynchburg for lunch tomorrow. I said yes.

The next day the two of us had lunch at Howard Johnson's restaurant. After I explained the process that I use to save money and time when building a church, he was intrigued. He said that his co-pastor, Jim Soward, the man he relied on most for construction decisions, was out of town for the rest of the week. He asked if I could return the following week and meet with him and Jim.

The next week, I made the same presentation to Jerry and Jim. "What do you think?" Jerry asked Jim. Jim's answer was, "I believe we can save about 20%." Jerry said, "That's what I thought. Let's do it."

They both looked at me. "Should I meet with a committee?" I asked.

"You just did," Jerry answered. I asked, "Who is authorized to sign the contract?" Jerry said, "I am." I reached for my brief case and took out a contract, filled in the blanks, and Jerry signed it. Jerry was never a man who was reticent to make decisions.

We broke ground on the Thomas Road Baptist Church worship center a few months later. The building was completed 14 months after that. The last Sunday of June 1970 was the 14th anniversary of the founding of Thomas Road Baptist Church and was the first service in the new 3,280-seat sanctuary. There were more than 5,600 people vying for seats that day.

Jerry and I became best friends. I was constantly doing projects with and for Jerry, and I continued to build churches. Each time there was a pastor's conference at TRBC, I was there. At the end of the conference, Jerry would call on me to come to the platform and pray the benediction.

Jerry would always say to the crowd, "While Duke is coming up here, I want you to look around at this beautiful building. Duke is the one who built it. If you are thinking about or planning a building program, talk to him before you leave here tonight." After I prayed, I just opened my notebook and took names. That solved my cash flow problem for another year. That is how I built more than 200 church buildings.

I really can't remember going to work for Jerry Falwell. We would be sitting around talking and dreaming and a project would come to mind and Jerry would say, "That's a good idea. Why don't you take a run at it?"

In the spring of 1971, TRBC had their annual stewardship campaign and banquet. Over breakfast, Jerry, Jim Soward, and I talked about the stewardship campaign and its success and how every church could do the same thing if they only knew how.

Jerry looked at me and said, "Why don't we write it up and you sell it to them?" We spent the next two days writing the program. I had a graphics firm design the materials and I began the marketing. We conducted the program in more than 50 different churches. The program was called *Above and Beyond*.

-15-

THE RIDE CONTINUES

The year 1971 was also the year that Jerry Falwell founded Liberty University. It was then named Lynchburg Baptist College. It began with 154 students and the early growth was incredible.

There were many factors that contributed to the growth of the college. Jerry's origin as an Independent Baptist was a significant factor. There were a number of Bible Colleges in the United States that were similar in

I Love America Rally on the Steps of a State Capitol

theology and practice that were supported by Independent Baptist churches, but there were no liberal arts colleges. LBC filled that void.

At the same time, the liberal arts colleges that were affiliated with the Southern Baptist Convention were perceived by many SBC pastors as becoming liberal in their core theology. Jerry Falwell's college became known far and wide for belief in the inerrancy of the scriptures, the deity of Christ and His death as atonement for our sins, His bodily resurrection, and His promised second coming. These were the very doctrines that separated SBC pastors from their own alma maters.

Both groups wanted a place to send their young people who wanted to be doctors, lawyers, and business professionals. Before long, Lynchburg Baptist College became the college of choice for Christians everywhere.

America's bicentennial was celebrated in 1976. In honor of that celebration, the the school was renamed Liberty Baptist College and later Liberty University. During the bicentennial year, Jerry decided to take Liberty University to America. He took a team of 70 students to the capitol steps of 47 states to perform a patriotic musical, written by Don Marsh, entitled *I Love America*. Thousands of local pastors would come with their congregations to see and hear the program.

Jerry would speak and call attention to the moral issues that both state and federal governments were politicizing. In many of these events, Jerry would ask me to go in advance and get the pastors mobilized to bring their people to the event. I would also arrange for transportation and accommodations for the team.

Out of the *I Love America* state capital events, the idea for the Moral Majority emerged. The evangelical pastors of America were awakened to the fact that 70% of the people who called themselves born-again Christians were not even registered to vote and the only way for positive change in America was through the ballot box.

Jerry knew that in order for the alliance to be effective, a broad coalition of churches would be needed. That would mean Catholics, Mormons, Jews, Pentecostals, Seventh Day Adventists, and pastors of all denominations would have to be included. An ecumenical partnership like this was abhorrent to many of the Independent Baptist pastors and leaders with which Jerry had been fellowshipping. He knew he would get a lot of criticism from them, but he knew in his heart that he was doing the right thing.

-16-

THE MORAL MAJORITY

The first meeting of the Moral Majority was in April 1979 at the Indianapolis Baptist Temple. There were about 2,000 pastors, priests, rabbis, and bishops in attendance. As the meeting was called to order, the first words from Jerry's mouth were, "Under ordinary circumstances, I would not be caught dead on the same platform with some of you and if the truth were known, many of you feel exactly the same way about me. But we are not here to discuss theology; we are here to save a nation. After that, we can go back to fighting amongst ourselves."

Laughter and applause broke out across the crowd. Everyone there knew of the seriousness of the plight of our republic. Jimmy Carter was president, inflation was at an all-time high of 16%, interest rates were 22%, and unemployment was at an astounding 10% with a 70% marginal tax rate.

Before long, more than seven million people affiliated

Falwell speaking at a Ten Commandments rally at Alabama Capitol

themselves with the Moral Majority, or as the media dubbed it, *The Religious Right.*

In November of 1979, Iran took 52 Americans hostage and held them for 444 days. America was looked upon by many as a helpless giant. The hostages were released at noon on January 20, 1981, just as Ronald Reagan took the oath of office for the presidency.

Exit polls in the 1980 presidential election indicated that 28% of the people polled were first-time voters and were encouraged to register to vote by their pastor or materials received from the Moral Majority.

Ronald Reagan was elected as the 40th president of the United States by an overwhelming majority.

From 1979 until 1985, Jerry Falwell spoke somewhere every day. Many days he would speak at a pastor's breakfast in one city, a luncheon in another city, a dinner and a rally in a third city, then fly back to Lynchburg and begin again the next morning. He was averaging between 250,000 and 300,000 miles each year.

Building a support base through television, radio, direct mail and media appearances was the key to raising funds for buildings and operating costs for Liberty University. The Old Time Gospel Hour was the broadcast arm of Thomas Road Baptist Church and had been since the late 1950s. Jerry was becoming ubiquitous on the national media scene and that translated to higher viewership of the Old Time Gospel Hour. The support base grew exponentially.

During this time, there was a lot of media attention wherever Jerry went. This attention drew a different kind of crowd to many of the events and made us take security seriously.

-17-

THE PIE INCIDENT

In 1982, Jerry was to speak at the Bible Baptist Fellowship's national meeting at the Will Rogers Coliseum in Fort Worth, Texas. We arrived early and went to a holding room. I left him there to check out the auditorium and the route we would take to the stage.

During this period, we were getting about 50 threats per week on Jerry's life and we were taking a lot of precautions. There were always pro-abortion and homosexual protesters at every advertised Jerry Falwell speaking engagement. This was no exception. Outside the building, we were greeted by about 200 sign carrying, shouting protesters.

When I looked in the auditorium, there were about 3,500 people. I was pleased to see that the house lights were on and the present speaker did not have a spotlight in his eyes. We wanted Jerry to be able to see the faces of his audience, and for security, we wanted to see movement in the building. Jerry was introduced, and like so many times before, people started to move toward the stage with cameras to get a closer photo.

Just then, the house lights went down and a spotlight was put on him. David Heerspink and Tim Vaughn, two security people traveling with us, immediately positioned themselves in front of the stage facing the audience so they could better see a threat.

I ran backstage to tell the lighting tech to turn up the house lights and kill the spot. He refused, telling me this was better for television. While he and I were in a heated discussion, I saw an object coming from the floor headed right for Jerry's head. It was a pie.

Jerry saw it coming over the foot lights and dodged just enough so that it hit him on the shoulder instead of the face.

I turned to the tech and told him that one of us was going to turn the house lights on and kill the spot. I suggested that it be him because I might break something.

A female, wearing a cape, and a male companion had made their way to the front along with the people wanting a photo. She had a pie hidden under the cape. From the edge of the stage she was less than 10 feet from Jerry when she pulled the pie from under the cape and let it fly. She had a good arm; she almost hit him in the face.

Tim Vaughn was standing about 8 feet from her when she threw the pie. He took two giant steps and dove to tackle her around the waist. She saw him coming and tried to duck under him. She ducked just enough for Tim to almost take her head off. She was close to being unconscious when he brought her up the aisle. I came around from backstage and met him about half way to the lobby. I told him to go back and stay with Jerry and let me take the woman to the lobby.

As I took her from him, she started coming around and began screaming. I placed my left hand over her mouth and she bit me and would not let go. To get her to release her bite, I placed my folded right fist on her ear and forcefully twisted it until she let go. I assume she has a cauliflower ear to this day.

Back at the stage, her male companion was shouting and fighting with people who were trying to get him away from the stage. He had both hands over the edge of the stage with his fingers clamped to the footlight trench. David Heerspink moved in behind him, reached around and hit his right arm straight up, grabbed his thumb, and rotated the hand and arm around to his back. As the man's arm came around, he moved in such a way that his arm snapped like a shot. As he screamed in pain, David dragged him up the other aisle to the lobby and met me with his accomplice.

When we reached the lobby, we looked around for a policeman and found none. We had these two people and didn't know what to do with them. I told David that I had an idea. We took them around to the back of the building, stuffed them into a large garbage dumpster.

We went back into the auditorium and saw that Jerry had pulled his jacket off and was preaching in his shirtsleeves. One of the stagehands came and asked if I was Duke. He said Dr. Falwell had told him to give this jacket to Duke. I spent the next 30 minutes in the restroom getting key lime pie out of Jerry's jacket.

As we were leaving the property, a police officer came to Jerry and asked, "Who put those people in the dumpster? They want to press charges." Jerry said, "I thought that some of your men took those people out." The policeman smiled and said, "That's pretty much what I thought you would say." He looked at me, smiled and winked, then said, "You all come back to see us, here.

Jerry, Macel and the Bushs at the White House

-18-

EVENTS FOR FRIENDS

With such a large and growing support base for the ministry and the Moral Majority, I suggested to Jerry that we do a series of banquets for Friends of Liberty around the country. This would give him a chance to meet people face to face and ask them to become regular donors to Liberty University.

In the next 18 months, we held 91 fundraising banquets. The least attended was 650 people and the largest was 3,700. Besides the immediate funds, we asked people to donate through wills, annuities, and bequeaths. We were notified of nearly $51 million that was put into wills and trusts from those banquets. Later, during some difficult financial times, nearly every month, we would receive a call from an attorney somewhere stating that one of his deceased clients had put Liberty University in his or her will for a bequeath.

During this time, Jerry was like Superman. His energy level was higher than any three men I had ever met. He was tireless. Almost always, we would land the plane after midnight and Jerry was up at 5:45 a.m. ready to go again. The only days he was not on the road were Saturday and Sunday.

Jerry never missed preaching twice on Sunday at TRBC. Above all, Jerry Falwell always saw himself as the pastor of a small town church. He performed weddings almost every Saturday, and if a member of TRBC died, Jerry made every effort to conduct the memorial service. Many times the service had to be scheduled at 9:30 or 10 o'clock in the morning so he could fly out to the next speaking engagement right afterward.

I remember one Saturday that Jerry performed three weddings and conducted four funerals in the same day. He later said he was afraid that at the end of the wedding, he would say, "the service will continue at the gravesite."

In 1984, President Ronald Reagan announced that he would seek a second term. Jerry Falwell planned an event in Washington, D.C., to coincide with the upcoming national election. The event was held in the new

Washington Convention Center. In fact, this was the first
event in the new facility. The event was called *Baptist
Fundamentalism '84.*

It was reported by D.C. media that more than 26,000
people were in attendance. The final day began with
Senator Jesse Helms at breakfast, Vice President George
Bush in the afternoon, and President Ronald Reagan in
the evening. To my knowledge, that is the most powerful
lineup of speakers at a single day's event in history.

They all came because Jerry Falwell asked them.

The successes of the Moral Majority are well chronicled
and documented. Some of the people who played major
roles in those world changing days are not so well known.

Ron Godwin ran the day-to-day operation of the
Moral Majority. Bill Faulkner was the early publicist during the *I Love America* state capitol steps programs.
Duane Ward, during the early 1980s, was the one who
managed Jerry's media appearances and publicity. During
that time, Jerry Falwell was the subject of thousands of
print articles, TV and radio programs, and was on the
cover of many magazines, including *Time* and *Newsweek.*

Ron Godwin went on to help start the Washington
Times Newspaper, which became the best conservative
newspaper in the country. In fact, it is the second most
quoted newspaper in America, second only to the *New
York Times.* Ron later moved back to Lynchburg to play a
major role at Liberty University.

For many years, Jerry Falwell, Ron Godwin, Edward
Hindson and I would eat lunch together virtually every
day. Some people called us a fellowship; I looked at us as
a brotherhood.

-19-

THE TOUR BUSINESS

Iwas traveling constantly. I was working with Jerry, building churches, and acting as a consultant to other ministries. Atlanta was home from 1975 to 1990.

I was not only working with Jerry Falwell, I was using many of the things that I was learning from him to help other ministries and churches. One such ministry was a television outreach in Florida, called *God's News Behind the News*. The host was Ray Brubaker.

We were holding a series of fundraising banquets around the country and I suggested to Ray that he hold a high donor event somewhere. After some discussion, he asked, "Duke, where is the best place to hold a high donor event?" I said, "The Hilton Hotel in Jerusalem, Israel."

He asked me to explain that to him. I told him, "If you take a group of people who are your best supporters to Israel and spend 10 days showing them the sacred sites of the Holy Land, you will become their spiritual leader as never before." I continued, "On the last night of the tour, you should have a dress up banquet at the hotel. Let the men wear suits and ties and the ladies long dresses. Make it a gala affair. At the banquet, show a multi-media presentation of your ministry; where it was, where it is right now, and where it can be next year with the help of everyone there that night.

"Then distribute commitment cards to everyone and ask how much they will give in the next 12 months." I said, "If you do it right, you will raise enough money for next year's budget."

He asked if I could arrange all of that for him. I said, "Certainly." After all, I had been to Israel one time.

I have been in the tour business ever since. Carlene and I have both been to Israel 57 times. We have taken thousands of people to Israel. We have taken many large groups for a number of ministries.

The largest group was in January of 1999 when we took 1,500 at one time. There were 900 Liberty University freshmen students and 600 of their friends and family.

People always ask Carlene to tell them how she kept up with 1,500 people. She says, "I didn't have 1,500 people—I had 32 busses. I can keep up with 32 busses."

Being tour operators is one of the most satisfying things in which Carlene, Kim, and I are involved. Seeing the reaction of Christians who see Golgotha and the Garden Tomb for the very first time is amazing. I often say that before a person visits the Holy Land, he or she reads the Bible in black and white. When you walk there, you read it in Technicolor.

Jerry and I made about 20 trips to Israel together. We met with heads of state and citizens of all kinds. Jerry was greatly admired in Israel for his unwavering support of the Abrahamic Covenant.

-20-

LYNCHBURG

In 1987, I was approached by one of the largest construction firms in America to set up and manage the business development of a division that would build only church buildings. They gave me the title of Vice President and Development Manager.

Our division was constructing between $60 - $80 million dollars per year in church and church-related buildings. We built the 10,000-seat worship center for First Baptist Church of Jacksonville, Florida. We also constructed many buildings on the campus of Liberty University, including the Williams Football Stadium, the Vines Center Basketball Arena, the three-story addition to the DeMoss Learning Center and a six-story dorm.

In 1991, Bob Street, the owner of the company, died of ALS (Lou Gehrig's disease) and the company was sold to a British firm. Overnight, we went from being the fourth largest general contractor in America to one of the largest construction companies in the world. The culture and the vision of the company changed immediately.

Although my division was doing about $80 million dollars in annual revenue, it was a drop in the bucket compared to the size and complexity of the overall business enterprise. I was working for a group of people who did not even know how to spell church and had no interest in building one. I could see instantaneously that I was going to be a product of downsizing, so I quit instead of giving them the satisfaction of firing me.

As mentioned earlier, in 1981, Carlene and I accidently got into the wholesale tour business. I believe that God doesn't trust me to make decisions on my own. I just wake up one day and find that I am doing something I didn't plan for.

We specialized in taking groups to Israel and surrounding countries. So as I left the church construction business (as it turned out, I was not out of the business entirely) we decided to go into the tour business full time.

The next decision was where we were going to live. We could run the tour business from anywhere.

We had lived in Charlotte for more than two years. That was the home office of the construction company. For some reason, Charlotte never felt like home to us.

Although I had spent so much time in Lynchburg working for Jerry, and Kim attended and graduated from Liberty University, we never lived there. We decided against moving back to Atlanta and Houston.

One Friday, we decided to drive to Lynchburg for the weekend. On the way, Carlene and I both said, almost simultaneously, "Maybe God is leading us to live in Lynchburg." When we arrived at our hotel, we got a newspaper and looked for houses. Because Kim is in a wheelchair, we had some special needs in a house. That night, we found a house that seemed to fit our needs. We saw it the next morning and two weeks later we were living in it.

A few weeks after we moved, I got a call from Jerry to meet him for lunch. Over lunch he said to me, "I need an executive assistant and you're it. I have an office, a phone, and we can share a secretary. You started at 8:00 o'clock this morning. Do you have a problem with that?"

I said, "Jerry, I'm in the tour business."

He said, "Carlene and Kim are in the tour business. You work for me."

"Ok," I said, "But I still have to be free to do other things that I am already involved in."

He said, "No problem, you've always been able to juggle things."

Working that closely with Jerry was incredible.

When people learned that I traveled with Jerry

Falwell, they would ask about the exotic places we went, the interesting things that would happen, the important people we would meet, and the wonderful places we would eat. Obviously, we did travel to great places and, indeed, we constantly met famous people.

-21-

NEW ORLEANS

One day, a few years ago, Jerry Falwell was scheduled to be the keynote speaker at the Pastor's Conference during the National Convention of the Southern Baptist Convention in New Orleans.

Three things happened that day that defined the man Jerry Falwell.

Above all, he was a people person. He genuinely liked people. Secondly, there was not a pretentious bone in his body. Thirdly, it was often said about him that what you see is what you get. In many ways, he was just plain Jerry. Those were qualities that made him a great pastor.

We had a small late breakfast that day, because of a pastor's meeting that Jerry had to attend. About 2:00 p.m., Ron Godwin, Ed Hindson, Jerry Falwell and I took a taxi to Café Du Monde, a famous outdoor French coffee house, where we met other pastors and their families.

We were seated around a large table with other pastor friends and their families when a boy about 10 years old came running around the table carrying a large tray of beignets and dumped them on Jerry's back. His black suit was covered with white powdered sugar from his shoulders to the bottom of his coat.

Needless to say, everyone was stunned. The boy was
in shock, his mother was almost in tears, and his father,
who was a pastor, started to chastise his son.

Jerry said, "Don't worry about it. We can get this out.
It's no big deal."

I spent the next 30 minutes in the bathroom with wet
towels getting the powered sugar out of the jacket. When
I brought the jacket back to the table, Jerry was sitting at
another table talking to the boy that spilled the beignets
on him. They were having a great time together talking.
Jerry told the boy he wanted to see him in eight years at
Liberty University.

Jerry never mentioned the beignets again.

Later we were walking around Jackson Square meeting and talking to the street people. As we crossed the
street in front of the large Catholic church on the square,
we saw a man sitting on a stool playing a violin. In front
of him, on the sidewalk, was a box about 24 inches long,
about 18 inches wide and 6 inches deep.

Lying in the box, sound asleep, was a yellow dog.
Lying on top of the dog, also sound asleep, was a black and
white cat. Sitting on the cat, just looking around, was a
mouse. In front of the box was a hand-painted sign that
read, "Can't we all just get along."

Jerry laughed out loud and said, "Now that's creative."
He then reached in his pocket and pulled out $20 dollars
and gave it to the man playing the violin.

After a while, Jerry said, "I'm hungry. Let's go find a
McDonalds."

Jerry Falwell was a simple eater. I often said, "Jerry
loves anything you can put in a bun."

We were all shocked. I said, "Doc, I can't believe you

said that. We're in New Orleans!" He said, "You mean that they don't have McDonalds in New Orleans?"

"New Orleans is the city with the greatest restaurants in the world. Surely you don't want a hamburger."

He turned to all of us and looked sufficiently chastised and said, "Ok, ok, where do you guys want to eat?"

Ron Godwin and I both said, "Let's go to K-Paul's."

Jerry said, "K-Paul's—what's that?"

I answered, "It's a restaurant owned by Paul Prudhomme, the chef who is credited with inventing blackened Cajun food."

"Ok," he said, "What do they have?"

I said, "Cajun seafood."

"Seafood," he exclaimed. "You mean like fish and shrimp?"

"Yes," I said, "fish, shrimp, crawfish, crab, and other great stuff like that."

Jerry was always using phrases to be jokingly contentious.

"Not me," he said. "My dog won't eat that stuff and I never eat anything my dog won't eat."

Ron Godwin said, "Well Doc, your dog was not invited to this party and Duke, Ed, and I want to eat at K-Paul's."

With that, he grumbled and said, "Let's go."

When we arrived at K-Paul's, we were shown to a table near the rear of the restaurant. When the waiter appeared to give us menus, he looked at Jerry and exclaimed, "My God, you're Jerry Falwell. I watch you all the time. Can I have your autograph?" Jerry said, "Sure."

The waiter shoved a menu toward him to sign. While he was signing, the waiter added, "Mr. Prudhomme is in

the kitchen. Is it all right if he comes out to meet you?"
Jerry said, "I would be delighted."

In a few minutes, Paul introduced himself and sat at
the table with us. We talked about different things like
business, the weather, and politics. Finally, he said, "Jerry,
I think God must have sent you today. My wife died
about 18 months ago. I have good days and bad days.
Today has been an especially bad day. Would you mind
praying with me?"

Jerry said, "Paul, I'll be honored." Jerry stood and they
went to the back of the building for a little privacy and
had a word of prayer. I looked back toward them and saw
Jerry, with his arm on Paul's shoulder, praying and Paul
was weeping. As they came back to the table, Paul was
wiping his eyes with his apron.

Before long, the waiter came back to take our order.
Ron and I each ordered blackened red fish (it was to die
for, incidentally). Ed Hindson ordered crawfish. We all
looked at Jerry, and he, without hesitation, said, "Bring me
some chicken fingers."

Paul excused himself for a few minutes and he went to
the kitchen and personally prepared possibly the only
order of chicken fingers ever served at K-Paul's Cajun
Restaurant in New Orleans.

Like I said, "What you see is what you get."

-22-

FIRECRACKERS

Jerry was always a practical joker and he loved firecrack-
ers. When we first met, Thomas Road Baptist Church

was meeting in the sanctuary that was built in 1964. It was full to capacity from the very first service.

To reach the door that leads to the platform from Jerry's office, it was necessary for him to pass by a ladies restroom. Some Sunday mornings, just before the service, Jerry would walk by on his way to the platform, open the ladies restroom door a little and toss in a lighted firecracker. The boom echoed off the concrete walls as ladies would come out of the door, saying, "Jerry, I'm going to get you."

For years, the ladies talked about this and laughed. That was a great memory of a man they adored as their pastor.

He loved to carry small stink bombs in his pocket. Sometimes he would drop one on the floor, step on it, and walk away. The people behind him were trapped in the smell and didn't know where it came from.

One night, Jerry was to speak at a banquet in Huntsville, Alabama. There were about six of us walking through the lobby of the hotel when Jerry dropped one of the stink bombs and stepped on it, thinking it would release its vile odor in the midst of the staff people right behind him. Unfortunately, a TV reporter caught him just as he stepped on the bomb and put a camera in his face and began asking questions. Jerry stood there and answered the questions with tears running down his cheeks. The smell was horrible.

-23-

NRB AND THE PICK-UP TRUCK

The National Religious Broadcasters (NRB) is an association of gospel ministries, churches, relief organizations and media outlets that are banded together to assist each other in all aspects of electronic media.

The organization began many years ago when radio was the primary media for spreading the gospel. As television came of age in the 1950s, new names began to dominate the religious airways; names like Billy Graham, Rex Humbard, Bishop Sheen, and Jerry Falwell.

After Ronald Reagan's election in 1980, the dominant media and career politicians in Washington gave the majority of the credit (or blame) to the Religious Right and gave credit for the emergence of this group to the Moral Majority and Jerry Falwell.

During the presidential campaign, Jerry invited Ronald Reagan to speak at Liberty University. To keep it from appearing to be a special favor to Jerry Falwell, the NRB became the sponsor of the event, and the event was held at Liberty University. Everybody benefited. Ronald Reagan became president, Liberty University became a well-known university and the NRB came of age as a major player and lobbyist in Washington.

Jerry Falwell soon became a board member of the NRB.

There are many NRB stories that can be told, some about people and others about events. Some are sad and others are funny. One such Jerry Falwell story happened as we were trying to get to the Opryland Hotel in Nashville for an NRB board meeting.

The board meeting was scheduled for 8:00 a.m. on Monday morning. Obviously, Jerry preached at Thomas Road Baptist Church Sunday night, so we departed Lynchburg very early the next day.

There were six people on board the aircraft, including Carlene. She was going because our tour company was exhibiting at the convention. The weather was perfect. There was not a cloud in the sky. As we got closer to Nashville, the tower was reporting heavy fog at the airport. We could see downtown Nashville and for miles around, but the airport was totally shrouded in fog.

There was a small airport about 40 miles north of Nashville that was clear, so we decided to land there. We landed at about 6:30 in the morning. Nothing was open. The small airport office was closed. The hangars were locked up and there was no place to rent a car.

I saw a church bus parked in front of a house about a block away. I knocked on the door of the house and asked the lady who answered about the bus. I told her that Jerry Falwell needed a ride to Nashville and asked if we could borrow it. She said that her husband was a deacon at the church and would have no objection to us borrowing the bus, but he had the keys with him and he was in Nashville.

I thanked her and began to look around. I saw a pick-up truck parked in front of a building and the side door of the building was open. I ran to the door of the building and shouted to see who was there. A man answered. I told him the same story that I told the lady. He said that he needed his truck but his brother had a truck that we could use and he lived just around the corner.

He called his brother and the truck was delivered to us in about 15 minutes by a man who had obviously been awakened from a deep sleep. He was thrilled to let us use his truck.

The truck had seen better days. The Ford Ranger was at least 10 years old and had not been washed in a number of those years. The breaks squeaked and the shock absorbers were nonexistent.

Luckily there was a cover over the bed of the truck because the outside air temperature was about 25 degrees. Three of the guys had to ride on spread out newspapers in the back of the truck. Carlene was wedged between Jerry and me in the small cab.

The truck rocked back and forth because of the lack of shocks and each time we hit a bump, it was bone jarring. We looked like the Beverly Hillbillies as hundreds of people watched us arrive at the front door of the luxurious Opryland Hotel. Everyone there recognized Jerry Falwell as he manually rolled down the window on the passenger side and asked the bellman, "Where do you want me to park my limousine?" Everyone there laughed. Jerry Falwell had made a memorable grand entrance.

-24-

BAPTIST FUNDAMENTALISM '84

While the media was still reeling from the successes of the Moral Majority, Jerry decided to hold a major event in the bowels of the beast. He wanted an event unlike anything that Washington, D.C., and its elitist

Jerry introducing Ronald Reagan at BF 84 in Washington

media had ever experienced.

We planned a three day meeting at the brand new Washington Convention Center in April of 1984. The speakers would be pastors, religious leaders, members of Congress, and the Senate.

Jerry gave me the job of making it all happen. I had a staff of about 20 people. The build up to the event got the attention of the Washington media.

Three weeks before the event, Jerry called me around 2:00 a.m. one morning saying that he wanted to take 3,000 of the Liberty University students to Washington for the event. The next day, I chartered 85 busses, arranged for hotel rooms and the catering of 29,000 meals for 3,000 students plus faculty.

It was necessary to furnish transportation for everyone from their hotels to the Convention Center and back. I had those 85 busses, so I established a bus system with routes to and from 23 hotels.

The final day of the event was beyond belief and expectations. Senator Jesse Helms spoke in the morning session, Vice President George Bush spoke in the afternoon and President Ronald Reagan was the final speaker that night. The atmosphere in the building was electric. Jerry moderated the entire event and the media gave him top billing, right along with the President.

This was the first time that the President and Vice President ever appeared on the same day at an event.

The next day, the Washington Post had a great report on the event and reported that the building was packed with 26,000 people.

After I accompanied Ronald Reagan to the stage, I went down to the auditorium floor with Duane Ward and Nelson Keener. We looked around at the crowd, the stage, and the press area and said, almost in unison, "Son-of-a-gun, we pulled it off."

-25-

W.W.J.D.

The year 2000 was one of the fiercest political campaigns I can remember. President Bill Clinton was coming to the end of his eight years in office and his Vice President, Al Gore, was nominated by the Democratic Party to hopefully become his successor. Texas Governor, George W. Bush, was the Republican Party's nominee.

Because Ohio was such a pivotal state in the election, Jerry Falwell and I traveled their to meet with pastors and other leaders for the purpose of motivating them to get their constituents to register to vote.

Most of the time, the media never learned that Dr. Falwell had been in the state until after we left. That's the way he wanted it, because he knew that he was such a lightning rod that the media would make him the issue rather than the real reason he was there.

On the night before the election, Dr. Falwell and I were in Columbus, Ohio, where he was speaking at a local church. When they heard that Jerry was going to be there, the Columbus media was in frenzy. They insisted on a press conference.

After about 30 minutes of questions and statements, I said, "We have time for only one more question before he has to be on the platform for the service."

Jerry looked toward the print media from the local paper and indicated for him to ask the last question.

The reporter began by clearing his throat and began to speak. "Reverend Falwell," he said (when they start that way, you know something silly is coming). "Reverend Falwell, I see young people here at the church wearing bracelets with the letters W.W.J.D. Tomorrow is Election Day. Let's assume that Jesus was here in Columbus and walked into a voting booth. He would see one lever that reads Albert Gore and another lever that reads George W. Bush. W.W.J.D.—What Would Jesus Do?" How would Jesus vote?

Without hesitation, Jerry answered, "If Jesus was here, He would be King and we would not be voting. I must leave now and go preach." With that, he left the room. The reporter had a sick look on his face. He really thought he had Jerry in a tight spot where anything he said could be criticized.

-26-

FAMOUS PEOPLE

It has been said that you can best judge the importance of a man by who his friends are. I submit that you can also judge him by his enemies. Jerry Falwell was always an anomaly; he had many detractors, but few enemies. Virtually everyone who knew Jerry liked and admired him.

Outside of Lynchburg, Virginia, Jerry will be remembered most as the founder of the Moral Majority. The organization was created in 1971 for the purpose of bringing Christian people into the political process. For so long, Christians were taught that politics and religion don't mix. Therefore, most Christians never bothered to register to vote.

When Congress and the Supreme Court legislated and ruled on banning prayer in schools and the legalization of abortion, Christians felt that the government was trampling on biblical principles.

Jerry Falwell, Tim LaHaye, James Kennedy, and Charles Stanley began meeting with men of similar positions on these issues who they could support in the 1980 presidential election. When they spent a few hours with Ronald Reagan, they were confident they had found their man.

RONALD REAGAN
Ronald Reagan and Jerry Falwell became close friends. Reagan came to Liberty University in 1980 and invited Jerry to appear with him in campaign appearances.

Jerry was invited to the White House for bill signing ceremonies and other events throughout the eight years of

Reagan's presidency. Ronald Reagan never turned his back on his principles or his friends.

About four years before Ronald Reagan died of complications related to Alzheimer's; Jerry and former U.N. Ambassador Jeane Kirkpatrick were both speaking at an event in Washington, D.C. We were in the green room at the hotel waiting to be escorted to the stage.

Jeane told Jerry about seeing the former president a few days earlier and found him to be almost like his old self. Nancy Reagan had said that some days were much better than others, and this day was one of his best in a long while.

Jeane told Jerry that when she and the president were talking about one of the Republican Conventions where Jerry prayed, he said that the prayer set a positive tone for the whole week.

Ronald Reagan was Jerry Falwell's friend.

Reagan and Falwell in the Oval Office

Falwell with George H. W. Bush

GEORGE H. W. BUSH

When George Bush was chosen by Reagan to run with
him as Vice President, he was not pro-life. It was not that
he was passionate about his position; it was just that no
one had taken the time to calmly explain the real issues
instead of shouting at him and calling him a baby killer.

The President suggested to Jerry that he meet with
Bush over lunch and discuss this as a friend. It was not
long until Vice President Bush said publicly that he had
changed his position and was now pro-life.

In 1990, President George Bush was the commencement speaker at Liberty University. When Air Force One
landed in nearby Roanoke, Virginia, the President and
First Lady invited Jerry and Macel to fly on the Marine
One helicopter from there to Lynchburg.

Each Christmas during the Bush's term in the White

House, the Falwells were invited to the Bush family Christmas party. The former president invited Jerry and Macel to the opening of his library in College Station, Texas, and again to his 80th birthday party.

George Bush was Jerry Falwell's friend.

BENYAMIN NETANYAHU

Prime Minister Benyamin Netanyahu of Israel respected and appreciated Jerry Falwell for his unswerving dedication to the nation of Israel. Netanyahu was one of the first Israeli politicians to recognize the significance of the evangelical Christian commitment to the Abrahamic covenant. From the time that he was Deputy Israeli Ambassador to the United States, Netanyahu and Jerry Falwell continued

Jerry with Prime Minister Netanyahu in Jerusalem

their friendship until Jerry's death in 2007.

On the other side of reality, Yasser Arafat thanked Jerry Falwell many times for bestowing five full Liberty University scholarships to Palestinian young people per year. Jerry considered the educational opportunities he afforded them to be a possible investment in the peace process between Jews and Arabs. Arafat sent a letter of thanks to Jerry and told me, in a private meeting, to again give Dr. Falwell his sincere thanks. Jerry never met Arafat personally.

GEORGE W. BUSH

George W. Bush liked and respected Jerry. On a number of occasions, the President invited Jerry to witness the signing of legislation in which Jerry had a special interest. Jerry was invited to the Washington National Cathedral for the September 11 memorial service.

I was standing in the emergency room of the Lynchburg General Hospital at 12:35 p.m. on May 15, 2007. We had just been told what we already knew. Jerry Falwell had died.

My cell phone had been ringing for the last 30 minutes. Each time I answered, it was someone who genuinely cared about Jerry. They heard that he was taken to the emergency room and they wanted an update. I told each of them that I did not have conclusive information. But now, we knew. The next call was from a number I recognized and I answered immediately. It was Tim Goeglein, special assistant to President George W. Bush.

Tim's first question was, "Is he dead?" I told him, "Yes, they have not given an actual time of death yet, but yes, he is dead." Tim then asked if Mrs. Falwell would be available for a call from the President. I said yes and handed the phone to Macel.

George Bush was Jerry Falwell's friend.

OTHER FRIENDS

There were people on opposite ends of the political and spiritual spectrum that were good friends and admirers of Jerry Falwell. When Jerry went to the hospital the year before he died, **Senator Ted Kennedy** was the first person to call Jerry Jr. to find out how he was doing.

Jesse Jackson and Jerry would appear on TV programs for the purpose of strongly debating an issue or a cause. Occasionally the rhetoric would get loud. Jerry never lost his cool, or his pastoral approach.

When Jesse was severely criticized by the media about a moral failure, Jesse turned to Jerry for prayer. When Jerry had his first health issue about a year before his death, I got a call from Jesse. He said, "Duke, how's the big man?" I said, "Jesse, he's feeling pretty good right now, but because he was on a ventilator for a few days, his throat is so raw, he can hardly talk." Jesse laughed and said, "You tell him that I said America is much better off tonight because Jerry Falwell can't talk."

"Seriously, Duke," he said, "Tell him I'm praying for him."

Jesse Jackson was a friend of Jerry Falwell.

Al Sharpton and Jerry had a special relationship. Al wanted his daughter to come to Liberty and be under the mentorship of Jerry Falwell. However, his ex-wife would not allow it.

Whenever Jerry appeared on the **Larry King** show, during the commercial breaks, Larry would invariably ask

Jerry questions concerning Christianity and spiritual matters.

Jerry Falwell was on the **Phil Donahue** show more times than any other guest. Phil knew that when he had Jerry as a guest, his ratings would skyrocket. When Phil's CNBC show was in danger of cancellation, Phil called Jerry and asked him to come to New York and be his guest two weeks in a row, trying to get the ratings back up. It worked. Those two shows were the highest rated shows Phil had ever done. However, in the end, it was not enough to avoid cancellation.

Phil Donohue was Jerry Falwell's friend.

Others, I will list. I could give you a story about each one, but the book would be too heavy to lift.

Menachem Begin Prime Minister of Israel—He bestowed the Jabotinsky Award on Jerry Falwell

Anwar Sadat	President of Egypt
King Hussein	Monarch of Jordan
Yitzhak Rabin	Prime Minister of Israel
Aerial Sharon	Prime Minister of Israel
Henry Kissinger	Secretary of State
Clarence Thomas	Justice of the Supreme Court
Richard Nixon	President of the United States
Gerald Ford	President of the United States
Mike Huckabee	Governor of Arkansas
J.C. Watts	U.S. Congressman
Ted Kennedy	U.S. Senator
Tom Rose	Newspaper Publisher
Billy Graham	Evangelist
Sam Moore	Businessman
Sam Walton	Businessman

Arthur L. WilliamsBusinessman
Sean Hannity   Radio and TV Personality

Although Jerry Falwell was comfortable in the highest
level of business and politics, rubbing elbows with the elite
and important, he never lost the common touch. As I've
said before, Jerry saw himself, always, as the pastor of a
small-town church. His truest delight was being with
other pastors.

Dr. Jerry Vines, pastor of the First Baptist Church of
Jacksonville, Florida, was Dr. Falwell's closest friend in the
ministry. He and Franklin Graham were the main speakers at the memorial service one week after Jerry's death.
At the funeral, Vines said, "Jerry Falwell loved pastors. He
loved being with pastors and he loved mentoring pastors."
He continued, "There are scores of pastors who could say,
and be accurate, that they were Jerry Falwell's best
friend."

I could list Jerry's friends for days and I would still
leave someone out.

-27-

MACEL, I LOST MY PANTS!

In January 2001, Jerry was invited to the Bush/Cheney
Inauguration in Washington, D.C. Jerry was asked to
speak at a number of events and to participate in many media programs. I spent most of the week before working out
the schedules and planning transportation and lodging.

I can tell this story because Jerry told it on himself.

Jerry needed a tuxedo for the Inaugural events. I

reserved one for him at the local tuxedo rental store and set the time for him to come in and be measured. He was so busy that we had to reschedule the fitting three times. Finally, I said, "Jerry, you either take the time to get measured or you will have to appear in your pajamas."

By the time we got to the shop for the fitting, there was not enough time to do it right. They gave him a very large pair of pants that had a clasp and a ratchet on each side so when he put them on, he had to tighten the sides to fit. I bought him two pair of suspenders, one clasp, and one button, just in case.

As he was dressing to go to the Christian Coalition banquet at the Hyatt Regency Hotel, he did not realize that there were suspenders in the bag. He put on the pants and tightened the ratchet. It felt comfortable, so he thought he would not need suspenders.

When we arrived, we were greeted by over 3,000 people in the banquet hall. Our table was near the front, close to the stage. Person after person came by the table to speak to Jerry and many asked for his autograph. At the table was Jerry, Macel, Jeanie (Jerry's daughter), her son Paul, Ron Godwin, Carlene and me.

At the end of the dinner and program we were standing up to leave when Macel said, "Here Jerry, hold my coat. Jeannie and I are going to the restroom." As Jerry reached for her coat, Jeannie gave him her coat also. Jerry stood up awkwardly. I saw him reach for the waist band on the right side of his pants. I told him to give me the coats so he could hold his pants. As he grabbed one side of the pants, the other side gave way. Both of the ratchets had broken loose.

We began to walk toward the lobby. I was holding the

coats and Jerry was holding his pants up with both hands. Two ladies came up and stood on each side of Jerry and asked if a third lady could take their picture with him. Jerry said sure and put his arms around the two ladies and his pants hit the floor. He casually bent over and picked up his pants and started walking again. About twenty steps later, it happened again and with the same results.

Ron Godwin, Randy Smith, and I got Jerry by each arm and took him through the first door we could find. It was a kitchen ante-room. There we repaired his pants.

Later, in the limousine, Jerry said, "Macel, I lost my pants in the lobby while you and Jeannie were in the bathroom."

"You did not," Macel said.

"Yes I did, twice. Tell her, Carlene."

"He sure did," Carlene said.

"But it was no big deal," Jerry said, "my jacket was long enough to cover everything."

Carlene laughed and said, "Yes, everything was covered until you bent over to pick up your pants."

Jerry said, "I hope nobody got a picture. It will be in the National Inquirer tomorrow if they did."

Nobody got a picture, but enough people saw it that the word got around. The following week Jerry was to speak in Jacksonville, Florida at the annual pastor's conference. Pastor Jerry Vines heard about the incident and razzed Falwell unmercifully. Therefore, Jerry decided to tell the story himself to the 10,000 people in attendance. The people laughed for a good two minutes without stopping.

Jerry Falwell always enjoyed a good laugh at the expense of Jerry Falwell.

-28-

MONTEVIDEO

For a man who traveled constantly, Jerry Falwell hated to spend the night away from home. His attitude was that when he was out of town, he either wanted to be working or on his way home.

About once a month we would travel to the west coast to do television. We would leave at 6:00 a.m. from Lynchburg, make a connection in Washington, and arrive in Los Angeles in time to make the rounds of the different shows on which he was scheduled. After the last show we would return to the airport and take the red eye at 11:30 p.m. (2:30 a.m. Eastern Time) arriving home in Lynchburg at 10:00 a.m. That is a 28-hour day.

Once he was asked by a group to speak at a conference of 1,000 pastors in Montevideo. He readily agreed because he loved speaking to pastors. For some reason he thought Montevideo was in Mexico and was easy to get to and return the same night. By the time I explained to him that Montevideo was in Uruguay, South America, it was too late to cancel.

From the beginning, the inviting group was willing to pay all expenses. Jerry told me that he would go as long as we didn't have to spend the night. I told him that it was over 5,000 miles to Montevideo. He said as long as we were moving it wouldn't matter.

We departed Lynchburg on a private charter for Miami, Florida. There, we boarded a Brazilian airliner bound for Sao Paulo, Brazil, where we were to have a one hour layover. We landed and went to the gate for our connecting flight to Montevideo and were told that the flight was sold out and we must wait for the next flight in three hours. I told the gate agent that we had confirmed seats on the flight and showed her our tickets.

She explained that the practice there was to open the flight to everyone at the gate and when all seats were taken, the flight was full and everyone left at the gate must wait for the next flight.

Obviously, I disagreed with their practice and as people began to board the flight I demanded to see the supervisor. The attendant asked why and I continued to demand to see the supervisor. Eventually, the supervisor came. I explained that this man was famous and was expected to speak to thousands of people waiting for him as soon as we landed in Montevideo and we could not possibly wait for the next flight.

He said, "The flight is full and I do not care who the man is."

I smiled and said, "Now it's time for me to apologize to you."

He looked puzzled and said, "Apologize for what?"

I said, "I am about to ruin your day. If you think you may need to call security, now would be that time. This man and I are going to walk out that door, walk across the tarmac, and board that plane."

I took Jerry by the arm and we bullied our way through the door, marched to the plane, and climbed the stairs. As we entered the plane, I pulled the flight attendant's jump seat down and told Jerry to sit there, and I sat down on the floor in the aisle. The gate supervisor had followed us to the plane and was yelling and going crazy.

The captain came out of the cockpit to see what all the

fuss was. I told him we had confirmed seats and we were going on this flight. He demanded that we get off. I said no. He yelled at the supervisor to call security. I told him that he could call whoever he wished, but we were not getting off.

Jerry was laughing and having the time of his life. In frustration, the pilot reached over me and grabbed a passenger seated on the aisle and literally threw him off the plane. He looked at Jerry and said, "Sit there." He pointed to me and said, "You get off." I answered, "Where he goes, I go." He was furious.

Just then, a man tapped me on the shoulder and said, "Sir, I have a solution. My eight-year-old daughter has a seat next to me. I can sit in her seat and hold her in my lap and you can have my seat." The pilot looked at the two of us and shouted, "Done. Button it up and let's go."

We arrived in Montevideo two hours later. A car was waiting to take us to the hotel where we showered, shaved, dressed, and went down stairs where Jerry preached for 45 minutes to the most fired up and excited group of pastors I have ever been with.

As we walked out the front door of the hotel, our bags were already in a car waiting to take us to the airport where we boarded a private jet that took us to Buenos Aries, Argentina. Our flight back to Miami departed two hours later. We arrived in Miami the next morning about 7:00 a.m. The charter was waiting on us and flew us back to Lynchburg. The total elapsed time from Lynchburg to Lynchburg was 40 hours. Jerry went straight to his office and worked the rest of the day. He never considered that he was away from home overnight because he was on his way home the entire time.

Top: Duke, Kim and Carlene
Bottom: Duke and Carlene with the Falwells at Macel's birthday party

Top: Duke and Carlene With Sean and Jill Hannity
Bottom: Duke with Governor Mike Huckabee

Top: Counter Terrorism Training
Bottom: Carlene Duke and Kim with Charlton Heston

Duke with Henry Kissinger

Duke with Charles Stanley

Top: Duke with Ido on the Red Sea
Bottom: Duke Speaking to a tour group on the Mount of Olives

Top: Duke with Benny Hinn in Egypt
Bottom: Duke with Senator Brownback

Duke Introducing Governor Bob McDonnell

Top: Duke and Jerry with Governor Haley Barbour
Bottom: Duke, Jerry, John Hagee and Congressman J. C. Watts

Top: Duke, Jerry and Ronald Reagan
Bottom: Steve Forbes, Duke and Jerry

Top: Duke at the Great Wall
Bottom: Jerry and Duke

WOW! WHAT A RIDE

Top: Duke Speaking at Liberty University Convocation
Bottom: The Vines Center

Top: Duke, Carlene, and Ronald Reagan
Bottom: Duke and Jerry on a plane

Dr. Jerry Falwell giving Kim her diploma

Jerry Falwell speaking at Thomas Road Baptist Church

Top: Duke speaking at a luncheon
Bottom: Duke with George H. W. Bush

PART 3

TEA WITH TERRORISTS

-29-

SEPTEMBER 11, 2001

"December 7, 1941—a day that will live in infamy." These words were spoken by President Franklin Roosevelt to a joint session of Congress the day after the cowardly attack on the U.S. fleet in Pearl Harbor, killing nearly 3,000 men and women of the Armed Services.

Any person old enough to remember these words remembers exactly where they were when they heard them.

The story you are about to hear is true. I have changed the names of a couple of people to protect their anonymity and the safety of their families. I also will not go into exactly how I was able to set up this meeting; that would endanger another set of people who are dear to me.

As a student of history, I know that wars are, more often than not, a result of a dispute concerning economics. Only in the last half of the twentieth century have wars been fought over ideas and convictions. My time spent in the Middle East has taught me that there is an ideology that defies explanation. I have seen the results of suicide bombers. I have seen not only the carnage and devastation they sow immediately, but the social and political aftermath that paralyzes a nation.

The morning of September 11, 2001, I, like most Americans, sat glued to the television set wondering what on earth was happening. Who had declared war on my country and why were they doing it?

We had landed about 3:30 a.m. traveling from

Houston, Texas, where Dr. Falwell had spoken the night before. Traveling with us was Craig Winn, a businessman from Charlottesville, Virginia. Craig and I had become good friends over the previous two years because we shared a passion for history and enjoyed discussing philosophies and the causes and effects of world events.

About 10:30 a.m., while I was still glued to the television, Craig called to ask my take on the events at the World Trade Center, the Pentagon, and the field in Pennsylvania. He asked me, "Why are these people doing this? Why do they hate us and Israel so much? I tried to give him a 4,000-year history lesson about Isaac and Ishmael in about 90 seconds. He cut me off mid-sentence and said, "I've got an idea. I'll call you back after awhile," and he hung up.

Later that day, he called again and said, "Duke, you and I are going to write a book."

I said, "That's great. I have always wanted to write a book. What are we going to write about?"

He said, "It will be about a Navy Seal who gets caught in a terrorist incident and almost loses his life and the lives of all of his men. Then, like me, he wants to discover why Islam breeds such hatred."

He continued, "Much of the book will take place in Israel and I have never been there. I know that you have spent a lot of time in the Middle East and understand the culture. And, you have been to Israel more than 40 times. You need to help with the research and the writing."

I told Craig that I thought it was a worthwhile project and I would be happy to help. The next few months gave me an education that altered everything I learned in my study of history and it also made my blood run cold.

After many sessions discussing plot lines and local places of interest in the Middle East, Craig called on the first of December and said it was time for us to go to Israel. He wanted to meet and interview high Israeli government officials, intelligent officials, military officials and the average Israeli man-on-the-street. He further said, because I had met Yasser Arafat, and knew many people in the West Bank, that I could probably arrange for us to meet and interview their counterparts in the Palestinian Authority (PA). I told him this might be a little more difficult because the PA was at war with the nation of Israel.

Then, he laid a big one on me. Craig said, "Here's one that I am not sure you can pull off, but if anyone can, it's you."

He said, "I want to meet with Palestinians who have been involved in terrorist incidences where Israelis have been killed and these guys did the killing. I want to interview guys with blood on their hands."

Incredulous, I said, "You want me to set up a meeting with real terrorists."

He said, "Yes."

I answered, "Craig, I'm not sure I know how to do that."

He said, "Give it a try."

"I am not sure that I can pull that off," I said, "but I'll give it a shot."

Three days later, Craig Winn and I boarded an El Al Airlines plane for an amazing adventure. The first night in Israel was one of the most memorable I will ever experience.

-30-

ONE MAGIC NIGHT

I often wondered about my lack of emotion during my salvation experience. I have never doubted my salvation, not one time. But it bothered me that I was so analytical about it. Many times, I have led someone to the saving knowledge of Christ and they would weep for joy and almost shout about their happiness. I was always analytical about it. Things changed 45 years after I was saved. My flood of emotions finally came.

We arrived in Tel Aviv at 2:30 in the afternoon. Ido Keynan, a long time friend and former agent of the Mossad, met us and drove us directly to the Knesset Building in Jerusalem where we had four meetings scheduled with members of the Knesset and members of the Cabinet. The meetings lasted until about 7:00 p.m.

We stopped at Sammy's for dinner and proceeded to the Old City Wall. There was nothing like seeing the Old City Wall at night and because it was Craig's first time, I wanted him to see it all lit up.

We drove to the Jaffa Gate and Ido was giving the history of the Citadel Tower and other curious sites. We drove around the west side of the wall and viewed the New Gate and the Damascus Gate. There, we were stopped in our tracks by thousands of people in the street, on the sidewalks, and up against the buildings on each side of the street. They were shouting at each other, dancing, eating, and just milling around.

Ido said, "Oh, wow, I forgot. Today is the last night of

Ramadan. The Moslems have just broken the fast and they are celebrating. This is not the time for us to be here. As he began to back the car out of the crowd, Craig said, "Where is Golgotha?"

I said, "About two blocks straight that way," as I pointed toward the center of the mass of people. "We will see it tomorrow."

Craig said, "I want to see it now."

"Craig," I said, "That's not a great idea. See those people," I continued, "They are not friendly tonight and we would have to drive this van right through the center of that crowd. They will be right at the window, looking to see who is desecrating the celebration of their Holy day."

I said, "Craig, you don't look Arab, I don't look Arab, and Ido surely doesn't look Arab. This is not a good idea."

He said, "I want to see it now!" Multi-millionaires are not in the habit of hearing the word no.

I looked at Ido and asked, "What do you think?"

He reached down to his ankle holster, got out his Glock, ratcheted a shell into the chamber, put on the safety and stuck it in his belt. Without looking at me or Craig, he said, "Let's go."

We began moving very slowly through the crowd, blowing the horn to get the people's attention and ease through the mass of humanity. People would tap on the window of the van as we passed. They would shout at us for disturbing their celebration. We never acknowledged them as we looked straight ahead.

Two blocks later, I told Craig to look to the left, between that building and the bus station. "See the big hill in the back; it looks like the face of a skeleton. That's Golgotha. You can see why they call it Skull Hill."

As we continued by the bus station building, he looked back at the site again. There was a street lamp beside the rock face that stood in front of a small Moslem Mosque. The light from the street lamp was just enough to cast eerie shadows on the stone that intensified the look of a skull.

Craig said, "I want to go back there."

I said, "Craig, there are about 100,000 people in this street who don't like you. They will be as close as 100 feet from where we would be standing."

"I want to go there now," he said. I just looked at Ido and he made a u-turn and drove to the back of the station and parked right next to the guard rail in front of the rock. We all exited the van. Ido walked to the side of the van with his hand on his weapon to watch for intruders.

Ironically, we were the intruders.

I looked around to see if we were in any immediate danger. I could see and hear people in the street. They were milling around, shouting to one another, and buying sweets from street vendors. Occasionally you could hear some fireworks exploding. Thank the Lord, no one was paying any attention to us. We were totally alone, standing under the most amazing display of stars I have ever witnessed. Ido had always told me that Jerusalem is the closest place on earth to heaven. Tonight, I believed him.

Craig climbed up and stood on top of the guard rail. He leaned over and placed both of his hands on the rock face and began to weep. I watched as this multi-million-aire scion of business displayed a broken heart, standing in the place where his Savior died, paying the penalty for his sin.

At that moment, as I looked at the observation platform at the Garden Tomb next door, the notion struck me. I had stood on that platform more than 40 times looking at this rock, but this was the first time I had stood on the ground in front of it. If this is the place where Jesus was crucified (and I am convinced that it is), I could be standing on the very spot. There was about six inches of asphalt under my feet, but below that, there was soil that could have been the sponge that soaked up His blood as it ran down the wood of the cross.

I couldn't help but think of everything that happened that brought Him to this place that day. My mind started wandering. My thoughts went back, not 2,000, but 4,000 years. At first, it was like I was standing in the midst of a movie set, but there were no cameras or lights. It was as real as anything I had experienced. I was watching Abraham and Isaac as they climbed Mount Moriah.

Isaac's lineage, according to God's promise, was to include the Messiah. Therefore, when God told Abraham that He wanted him to sacrifice Isaac to prove his faith and obedience, Abraham knew that God would either stop him or God would raise Isaac from the dead. He knew that God could not go back on His promise or His covenant to the world.

I could see Isaac leading the donkey with firewood strapped to its back. I could hear him saying, "Dad, look at that ugly rock face. Wouldn't that make a great altar for the sacrifice?" He continued, "There's the altar, we have the wood for the fire, but where is the sacrifice?"

Abraham answered him, "God will provide Himself a

sacrifice."

After Abraham was stopped by the angel from sacrificing Isaac, he looked further up the mountain and saw a ram caught in the thicket. God had indeed provided a sacrifice.

That scenario, in front of that ugly rock, was a dress rehearsal for what happened 2,000 years later at Calvary; the very spot where I was standing that December night.

In my mind, the scene was changing. I saw myself standing on the same spot, this time looking up at Jesus hanging on a cross. He was beaten and bleeding; He had a crown of thorns pressed down so firmly on His head that blood was pouring down his face.

It was as if I was standing in the center of a stadium with thousands of people in the stands watching in horror. They were the great crowd of witnesses, the saints who had gone on before. I could see the angelic choir. They were not singing; they were weeping. Everyone was in shock because they did not understand what was going on. Here was God's only Son, looking skyward, saying, "Father, Father, why have you forsaken me?"

At that moment, Jesus had the sins of the whole world—past, present, and future—on His shoulders and God had to turn away because He is holy and cannot look upon sin. Jesus had volunteered to be the Messiah. He became the sin sacrifice offering and thus was the substitute for all who would put their trust in Him.

God painted this picture in Leviticus when a man was required to take the best animal in his flock to the Temple where it was to be sacrificed by the priest for the man's sin. It would have been easy for the man to have one of his servants take the animal to the Temple, but God insisted the man must take it himself.

It would have been easy for him to deliver the animal to the priest and slip out the back door, but God was clear that the man must stand there with his hands on the head of the animal while it was being sacrificed. God wanted that man to know, beyond any doubt, that the only reason the animal was dying was because of his sin.

That's what it means to have a personal savior.

That night in Jerusalem, as I saw myself standing in the middle of an arena, I knew that I was the only one there who truly understood what was happening and why. There I stood, with both hands on the head of Jesus, God's perfect lamb, when He finally said, "It is finished," and bowed His head and died. He was my substitute. If I had been the only person on earth, he would still have had to come and die, because I was a sinner. He was, without a doubt, my personal Savior.

That night, my floodgate of emotion was opened wide.

-31-

ENTERING THE WAR ZONE

It was 2:00 o'clock in the afternoon, December 12, 2001, just 3 months after 9/11. Our world, as we knew it, had changed forever. Security had been heightened everywhere. Israel's military was on high alert. Five days prior, the Israeli Defense Force (IDF) was forced to send tanks and troops to Bethlehem to arrest militants who had helped plan and execute two suicide bombings in Tel Aviv and Natanya. As the Israelis entered the area (through the same check point that I was about to enter), the Palestinians began firing on the tanks and tried to block the streets with cars. I was about to see the results of war up close and personal.

As we arrived at the check point between Israel and the PA, Ido said, "Duke, I have known Craig only two days, but you and I have known each other many years. In a lot of ways, you and Carlene are like parents to me, and Kim is as close to me as my real sister. I am having difficulty saying what I am about to say because of my respect for you, but I feel that I must say it. I know you are going to go through with this no matter what, but it is the craziest thing you have ever done.

"You're entering the twilight zone. You're headed to a place without laws. It's the domain of thugs—a place where hypocrites convolute Islam to justify everything they do. They'll kill you for a sheckle. Be careful what you say. And for God's sake, don't provoke them," said Ido.

"Whatever you do, don't let them take you too far in and make sure you're out by sunset." Ido had no idea how we were going to influence either of these decisions. Our hosts would be armed to the teeth. We were only carrying our ball point pens.

"This is your last chance. The border is just over that rise. Once more I ask, don't do this, this isn't your war, it's ours."

I slapped Ido on the leg. "I'll be fine. I've got too much to live for to be yanking these guys' chains. They think we are writers working on a book that addresses both sides. We are just going to ask questions. We'll be nice, pretend that we are sympathetic to their cause, and then bail out."

"I will drop you off in no man's land and then turn around and wait. Here is a cell phone that I know will work. Call me every thirty minutes to let me know you are still alive. I don't know what I can do if you're not... I'll just have to wait and pray."

As it turned out, the cell phone did not work where we had the meetings. Ido was wondering how he was going to tell Carlene if something bad happened.

We got out of the van and strode daringly into hell. It was a foreboding world of desolate buildings, barbed wire, cement barriers, armed guards, and olive trees struggling to grow in and around rubbish laden piles of rock.

We walked across the border, showing our passports to the Israeli soldiers. The border was teaming with Palestinians trying to enter Israel on foot and in vehicles. Cars were lined up about three blocks waiting their turn to confront the soldiers.

After crossing the border, we walked about a hundred yards south. I looked to the left side of the road and saw a man driving a green minivan. Right on cue, he flashed his lights three times and made a u-turn directly in front of us. The driver said, "You Mahmoud's friend?"

I replied, "Yes," and we got in.

Mahmoud was a Palestinian Christian, not a Muslim. Growing up in Bethlehem, he went to school and associated with many young people who became Islamic radicals. The Muslims were taught from birth to hate the Jews and Israel and to distrust Christians. This whole scenario put Mahmoud in a tight place. He was an Arab, so the Jews were suspicious; he was a Christian, so the Muslims were also suspicious. He had to go along to get along.

Twenty years ago, the population of Bethlehem was 80% Christian and 20% Muslim. Today, it is just the opposite. The PA is run by Al Fatah which is an outgrowth of the Palestinian Liberation Organization (PLO). Yasser Arafat founded the PLO and is now the President of the PA.

Mahmoud bought into the PA rhetoric. The leadership said they were fighting for all Palestinians, Muslims, and Christians alike, and he believed them. He signed up for Force 17—Yasser Arafat's palace guard, his personal bodyguards.

Joining Force 17 put him on the Israeli watch list. He was walking a dangerous tightrope. He was brought up in a good home. His father was a businessman who was known and respected by many Israelis. Mahmoud never got his hands dirty in the business of terrorism, but he knew a lot of people who did. To stay alive, Mahmoud made friends with everybody. That makes his, shall we say, Christmas card list, highly valuable to the Israelis. He was told that if he would scratch the back of the Israelis, they would scratch his.

If he gave his pal's names and addresses to the Israelis, they would let him and his family leave Bethlehem. He said no; something about being a traitor. So he was stuck. I'm guessing that no one on his Christmas card list celebrates Christmas anyway. Actually, they're all Muslims and they're in some rather interesting clubs. The whole world has come to know their names: Islamic Jihad, Hamas, the PLO's Al-Fatah, Hezbollah, and al-Qaeda. These were all a far cry from the Boy Scouts.

We were there to learn a lot more about Arafat and his

gang. Arafat was now a hero of the liberal press in Europe and the U.S. The UN had become his staunchest supporter. The sympathy of the world was turning against Israel and toward Arafat and the PA. In their eyes, he had changed from a terrorist to a statesman and the international community had grown tired of the U.S. and Israel calling him a terrorist. But the leopard hadn't changed his spots. That is why we went; to get firsthand knowledge of what was going on behind the façade.

In horror, we flinched as we caught our first glimpse of the war-ravaged town. Far too many buildings had been destroyed by the Israeli Defense Force.

To add to the surreal experience, we saw children, some as young as five or six, darting from boarded up buildings and out into the street. Seeing our Caucasian features, they turned and pointed their guns at the speeding van. They may have been toys, but we couldn't tell; they looked real. The youngsters, all boys, pulled back the action on their weapons, giving the appearance that they were chambering a round. All the while, we agonized, wondering why they had been left unsupervised in the streets. There wasn't an adult in sight. It seemed bizarre. Where were their mothers?

As he turned the corner, the driver slammed on the brakes, bringing the car to a screeching halt. We flew forward, almost hitting the dash. Then we saw them. Another group of boys were climbing out of a storm drain in the middle of the road. They, too, were armed. They rolled up their sleeves like they wanted to pick a fight. It was as if we had entered the Land of Oz.

But no, there was no Emerald City. No happy faces, no singing of songs, and definitely no prosperity. Block after block told an eerie tale. As we passed through what had once been a shopping district, I remembered this was a place that I had taken many groups on a pilgrimage to the birthplace of our Savior. It was abandoned, all locked up. Giant steel doors covered what had once been a beehive of activity.

"Why are all the shops closed?" Craig asked. "Is it a holiday?"

"There is no business. No jobs. No money. Nobody works anymore," the driver said matter-of-factly. Things were worse here by far than at the deepest depths of the Great Depression in America.

Passing street after street of sealed doors gave us a bad feeling. It is a fact that poverty breeds nothing but trouble.

The driver headed toward an open square. The buildings on all sides were blown to smithereens. Black smoke had stained their faces. Rubble covered the sidewalks and there was a haunting mixture of concrete and broken glass everywhere. A clash of cultures had turned this place into a war zone. And this was no distant memory. This wound was still open and raw; the injury hadn't had time to heal.

No one was working to clean up the rubble and debris. It was as if they wanted to remind the people who their enemy was and for the foreign press to send pictures of the suffering innocent civilians.

Suddenly, we were no longer alone driving down empty streets. While there were no other cars, certainly no tourists, it was now evident where all the workers had gone. They had a new vocation. Like the children before them, they were playing army. But this time there was no question as to whether the guns were real.

It was a motley collection of lost souls. Some were in army fatigues, others were dressed right out of GQ, and some were in tattered clothes. But none were wearing the flowing robes or turbans so reminiscent of Arabs in other parts of the world.

The guns they played with were as eclectic as the men carrying them. Russian Kalisnakov's, mixed nation Galiles, Israeli Uzi's and American M-16s with clips inserted. It all spelled trouble. The glares we received as we sped past this group needed no translation. We were infidels from the Great Satan, defiling their holy ground.

A few hundred meters past the town square, the van came to a stop. The driver opened his door, stepped out, and walked away. As he did, another Arab man rose up from behind a wall in front of us, walked behind the van, and then climbed into the driver's seat. Without saying a word, he put the car in gear, turned right, and accelerated away from the square.

-32-

MAHMOUD

The new driver said, "Hello Duke, long time no see."

I acknowledge Mahmoud's greeting and asked about his family. I also asked why he was not able to pick us up at the border himself. He told me that he was still on the Israeli wanted list because he would not collaborate with them.

As we drove, we saw a constant onslaught of milling

gunmen everywhere we looked. Then, not a moment too soon, the green van pulled over next to a three-story white rock building. Mahmoud, a large man, every bit of six foot five and three hundred pounds, got out of the van, opened the passenger door, and introduced himself to Craig.

"Follow me," he said with a voice that was clearly more gentile than his appearance. Mahmoud wore a disarming smile. Things were looking better.

We entered the large stone fortress of a building through a set of thick steel doors. At each turn we passed men who looked like bodyguards. Mahmoud, with us a step or two behind, turned right, descended a narrow set of stairs, turned right again and entered a large room in the basement.

The scene was right out of the movies. An eight foot long green Formica table had been placed in the center of the room. It was surrounded by seven or eight chairs. It was the only furniture in sight, not unlike an interrogation room. The ceiling was especially low, six and a half feet at most. The light fixtures were broken, bulbs and wires exposed.

Maneuvering around them, I managed to find a seat facing the door. Craig was to my left.

Mahmoud set the stage. He said, "Your first interview will be with Al-Fatah. I've arranged for you to meet their captain. He is in charge of the military wing for this region, the second largest in the country. He said he was bringing two of his top lieutenants. You'll have two hours to question them. After they leave, your next meeting is with Hamas, followed by Islamic Jihad and al-Qaeda."

It sounded like a terrorist delicatessen.

-33-

AL-FATAH

The first man entered the room hesitantly, probing the darkened corners of the basement. All the while, he continued barking commands into a small handheld radio. In Arabic, they made little sense to us, but his tone of authority was unmistakable.

Gradually, he made his way to the center of the room. He was now flanked by an officer, a diminutive yet handsome man dressed in smart looking military fatigues. Seconds later, a third man, tall and handsome, also in jungle green, slid in behind the other two. He was Hollywood handsome, with a strong chin, dark curly hair, broad shoulders, and a perfect smile. He canvassed the room.

It was obvious to me that the leader didn't much like his strategic disadvantage, having his back to the door. While they were in his territory, it was apparent Fatah had enemies.

Mahmoud introduced the leader by name, saying that he was a captain. But he did so with a warning, a stipulation that repeating his name would end the interview.

Craig and I said that we understood, making a pledge to keep all parties anonymous. We reiterated the fact that we simply wanted information.

With a nervous grin, the diminutive leader reached out and shook the hand of each of us. It was a surprisingly weak gesture. His hands were thin, even frail, and were swallowed inside mine.

Sitting with his back to the door, directly across the

table from me, he said, "I am the most wanted man in this
country." Maintaining a braggadocios tone, he continued,
"The Israelis Shin Bet has me at the top of their list."

"Why?" I asked.

"They think I'm responsible for the most recent killings."

I asked, "Which killings?" I was unconsciously wiping
my right hand on my pant leg. It was as if it was covered
in germs, as if the urge to kill was contagious.

"The settlers on the bus to Emmanuel," was his
answer. He smiled, turning to his lieutenants and sharing
the glory.

I had read about the incident in the Jerusalem Post.
"The people that were shot when they were getting off the
bus," I asked?

"Yes, we do not use suicide bombers. We are soldiers."

Craig asked, "Were you responsible for that?"

The leader's face erupted into another uncontrollable
grin. He wiggled in his chair and tried to look away. "I
will not tell you how many Jews I have killed."

"There have been many?"

He looked away again. He could not hold our gaze.

Mahmoud translated, turning the last statement into
a question. The captain nodded.

"He says yes," Mahmoud repeated, almost laughing at
himself. A nodding head was universal, as was the delight
that was still written all over his face.

The lieutenants shuffled in their chairs. They
preferred to pace. They, like their leader, were very
uncomfortable.

Craig decided to change the subject. We already knew

that terrorists killed; the question was why.

Craig began, "I noticed the uniforms. What organization are you with, and why did you join?'"

"Fatah," he said, "The majority of Palestinians belong, that's why."

"Who is the leader of Fatah?" I asked. I already knew the answer; this was for Craig's benefit.

"Arafat. I report to him," the leader said in a manner that questioned my intelligence.

Craig said, "I thought Arafat ran the PA."

"Fatah is the name the PLO has given to our mission. There is a political wing, like your political parties, and there is a military wing. These gentlemen are all from the military side. They are army men," Mahmoud explained.

"But we are not killing now," the leader said in a rather disappointed tone.

"The bus shooting you said you are wanted for—it was only two days ago."

"Yes, that was then. Arafat didn't ask for the cease-fire until yesterday."

"Were you involved in planning the shooting?"

"Yes, but not alone. We worked with Hamas."

"Hamas—I thought Arafat had just ordered you to put Hamas members in jail."

"Yes. That is why we are looking for them today."

"Yesterday they were your partner, and today they are your enemy?"

Following this line of reasoning, Craig asked, "If Yasser Arafat wakes up tomorrow morning and asks you to start killing again, will you?"

"Yes, of course."

Craig was dumbfounded. He had been told that

Yasser Arafat was now a diplomat, and that even if he had once been a terrorist, he had left that life behind. Now he was a peace-loving man only interested in serving his people by negotiating a settlement. He was even a Nobel Peace Prize winner.

"It's all your fault, you know," the diminutive leader said, breaking the silence. It would not be the last time we would hear that excuse.

"Extremists, fundamentalists, and radical Islam are America's fault—you and the Jews."

"Why?" we asked.

"First, you must know we are not like them. Fatah is not about extreme Islam. We are not committed to pushing the Jews into the sea. We just want them out of Palestine—out of our land—the land in which I was raised in occupation." The captain's tone was defiant, yet his words were reasoned. "Our goals are reasonable, so are our methods. We only want what is rightfully ours. They are the crazy ones."

He stopped to let that sink in. "They are still in the minority here but their numbers are growing very rapidly—very, very rapidly."

"Why?"

"You saw our town. No one is working. The Israelis have murdered our children. People are starving. And Hamas and Jihad have the money."

"What money?"

"Before I answer, you need to know how we are suffering. No one has worked for almost 16 months."

"The start of the last intifada, right?"

The actual meaning of the word intifada is uprising. It is a call to arms. Arafat had told his followers to step up the terrorizing of Israelis some time back and told them not to stop until they had achieved all of their political objectives. The blood bath that followed had left the parties deeply divided, wary of the other, and hateful. Barricades had replaced roads. Rhetoric had replaced reason. Death had swallowed hope.

"Yes, the intifada. Since that time we have suffered. The only way we can feed our families is with the help of other Arab nations. As a result, our people are thinking very bad thoughts—very, very bad thoughts."

"What kind of thoughts?"

"Killing. Poverty leads to Hamas. I am a Muslim. So are my men. We observe all of the holidays with our families, and we follow the traditions of our faith. But they do not think like us. They are crazy; more violent."

When men who are crazy enough to celebrate killing innocent people call another group crazy, they must be really crazy.

I saw the members of Fatah were growing uncomfortable with the line of questioning. "Let me ask a question," I broke in. They all looked at me. "As I understand it, you are trying to achieve three goals. There is not a chance of getting all three. Let me name the goals and you put them in the order of their importance.

"One—have a good economy where you can work and make money to feed your families and educate your children so they will grow up to have a better life than you have."

"Two—have some autonomy over the area where you live."

"Three—own the Holy Land."

The captain looked at his lieutenants. They appeared

to be having a rather heated conversation. It was as if they wanted to give the approved answer.

Their final response was translated by Mahmoud. "They say they want to own this land. It is where they were born. That is the most important thing to them. Next is autonomy so they can issue passports. Three, a good economy."

"Why," I asked, "is it so important for you to own the Holy Land? It has never belonged to you. For 400 years the Ottoman Turks controlled the land and there was more persecution and killing of Arabs than at any time in history.

"Then after World War I the British came and ruled until 1948. After that the Jordanians ruled until 1967 and then the Israelis until the Oslo Accord in 1993 when the Palestinian Authority and Arafat took over."

I had to wait for Mahmoud to translate. I continued, "Even your own officials admit that, under the Israelis, the Palestinians had the highest standard of living of any Arab people on earth. So why is it so important to own the Holy Land?"

The captain answered, "I was born here—that's why."

I said, "I was born in Texas, but there is no way I am ever going to own it."

Mahmoud looked at me and said, "I don't want to translate that."

I said, "Ok, let's talk about economy. You said that 80% of your people are out of work. Where do you get the money to live?"

"We get food and supplies from Saudi Arabia, Kuwait, United Arab Emirates, Iraq, and Ir...."

We could see that the captain had started to say Iran,

but had caught himself. The PA, through Fatah, had arranged to have $100 million dollars of Iranian weapons delivered to them, but the ship carrying the contraband was seized just a week before in the Red Sea by the Israelis.

Craig asked, "Is the money coming from the ruling families and the governments or is it coming from more secret sources?"

"Both."

"I have heard that these governments reward the families of the suicide bombers. Is that true?"

"Yes."

"How much and who pays?"

"We do not use suicide bombers."

"Yes I know. You use rifles. But do you know the size of the reward that is paid to the families of suicide bombers and from whom it comes?"

"The Syrian government pays $15,000 and the Iraqis $10,000. Iran also pays $10,000. But there is more. The families are taken care of for the rest of their lives. They are given better housing and the best food. The rest of their children get free university educations and the best husbands and wives."

"Sometimes they get even more," the handsome lieutenant said. "You know the little girl and mother that were shot by the Israeli soldier?"

I nodded. I had seen the film on CNN five or six years ago. It was a haunting example of what fear can do to a man's judgment in the midst of combat. To their credit, I recalled, the Israelis put the gunman in jail and apologized to the world for his behavior.

"Well, the woman's husband received over $1,100,000

from Saudi's Prince Fhad, Saddam Hussein, and the Sultan of Brunei. It was a reward for the good it had done our cause.

"The biggest money comes from Iran and Syria. But it only goes to Hezbollah and Islamic Jihad," he claimed. "The Syrians and the Iranians do not care about the Palestinian people. They only want to have agents inside Israel who will follow their orders. Agents that are properly armed. That is good for them.

"You Americans are often fooled by the Iranians, I think. You did not know why they offered to support the U.S. in Afghanistan and why they said they were against the kind of terrorists you were fighting there, especially when they were secretly funding more terrorists than anyone."

"So, why?"

"They knew that as soon as you were gone they would step in and control the government. Last time, the Pakistanis financed the Taliban. Now it is the Iranians' turn. They are all neighbors, you know."

The moment the Americans had lost interest in Afghanistan, that very thing had happened. As cesspools breed maggots, Islam breeds thugs. A new breed of warlords emerged out of the ruins, all too eager to wield Iranian weapons and kill their brothers in pursuit of power and money.

"You said earlier that Hamas, Hezbollah, and Islamic Jihad were growing very fast. When did they start growing?" we asked.

Mahmoud answered himself, "Islamic fundamentalism started here in 1988 with the first intifada. It took off following the Oslo Accords in '93 or '94. Now it is all about the money. You buy support here with dollars."

"How?"

"If you were out of work as 80% of the people here are,
would you let your children starve or would you accept
money to shelter and feed them? Do you think they just
give it away out of kindness?"

Mahmoud talked with the men in Arabic and sum-
marized in English. "If you accept their money, and their
food, you accept their authority and their way of thinking.
They all have people they assign to convince the families.
Soon they all start thinking whatever they want them to
believe. You go along or starve."

"You get what you pay for here. If you had money, you
could buy loyalty, too. Support comes from dollars.
Sometimes it's even your dollars.

"What do you mean?"

"Your government gives the Egyptian government
$2,700,000,000 a year. Some of that money comes right
here. The Egyptians don't like the Palestinian people,
either. Their money goes to Hamas and Islamic Jihad."

"What was it about the Oslo Accords that caused
militant Islam to grow?"

"The Israelis cheated. Their government was taken
over by the radical parties, the Shas and the Likud. They
returned to building settlements on our land."

"Did you know that we were trained by the Americans?"
the most handsome of the terrorists asked.

"We not only pay for you to kill Jews, we train you,
too?" Craig asked.

"Yes," the tall lieutenant replied. "My friend and I
were both trained in the United States, in Virginia, by the
CIA."

"We were there for forty days. There were 19 of us," the other, smaller man said.

"As we got ready to land they made us put our window screens down. We were blindfolded during the drive, too." The more handsome lieutenant smiled.

"You said it was in Virginia. What part?"

"It was a base of some kind. There were so many trees, giant trees, and a big body of water, a sea or a bay."

"Fatah gets lots of help from America. We are good friends."

"What does Fatah want?"

"We want pre-1967 borders. UN Resolutions 242 and 338."

I thought to myself, if they attack Israel and lose, they want what they lost back. I wonder if they won if they would be so eager to return the land they gained.

"Back at the end of the Clinton administration in 2000, the Palestinians were offered almost everything they wanted. Why did your leader, Yasser Arafat, turn it down?"

"Not everything," the captain responded. "We were not given Jerusalem."

"You were offered east Jerusalem. The agreement would have given you most of the West Bank and all of Gaza, too. Statehood and total independence."

They conferred among themselves in Arabic. "The refugee problem—that's why we turned it down."

Arafat wanted Arabs to flood back into what he called Palestine. The more the merrier. While those in Israel averaged six to seven children to a family, they were still outnumbered by Jews two to one. But if the immigration floodgates were opened, an estimated 5,000,000 Arabs

would be allowed entry, instantly putting them in the
majority.

Mahmoud was getting more nervous, now constantly
looking at his watch. The second set of terrorists was calling him on his cell phone asking if the coast was clear.
The first meeting had run a little long and thanks to recent
events there was a discord growing amidst the Muslim
militants. The first group, the PLO's Fatah, was hunting
the second group, Hamas and Islamic Jihad. The first had
to leave for the second to arrive.

Craig and I knew that it was all a charade. In previous
days we had talked to enough Palestinians to see that they
were playing a game. Arafat had come under pressure
from America and Europe to diminish terrorist killings.
Rather than admit his own party, Fatah, had been responsible, he blamed all the atrocities on Hamas and Islamic
Jihad. He promised the west that he would put the offen-
sive souls in jail.

In actuality, he had had his PA officers and Fatah jail
only a handful of foot soldiers. They were taken from
their homes with a promise of good food, a comfortable
stay, and a quick release. According to the Palestinians we
had met with, they were even told that the only reason for
the game was to appease the Americans. When Mahmoud
explained to the first group that they had to leave so that
the second group could come in, they all laughed.

-34-

HAMAS, ISLAMIC JIHAD, AND AL-QAEDA

A nd so it was. Within seconds of al-Fatah saying goodbye, we found ourselves shaking hands with an entirely different breed of terror. These fine folks were introduced as Islamic Jihad, Hamas, and al-Qaeda. Unlike their predecessors, their uniforms were not coordinated. They had evidently not been trained by the CIA, nor supported by the U.S. Government.

"How did you get the M-16?" was Craig's first question to the one from al-Qaeda.

Although I was intimately familiar with the weapon, it looked different and considerably larger and more deadly when it was just on the other side of the table from me.

"I can't buy an M-16 and I'm an American," Craig continued.

"Made in America," the Hamas member said proudly, patting the rifle. "Would you like one? I sold my land for this gun."

"Sure, I want one. How much?"

"I paid $2,500 for mine," he said. "But since the last intifada, the price has gone up. Now they're $7,000. The Jews sell them to us—black market."

Still fixated on the M-16, I asked, "Why do you need an assault rifle?"

"To protect myself from Israelis."

"I don't see any Israelis here, on this side of the border, so why are you armed?"

"I must be ready to protect myself. The Quran says

that we have to fight but that we should prepare first and not hurry into the battle."

"You know killing is not a hobby for us," the smallest of the Jihad members spoke.

"Then why do you do it? I assume you do. I mean, after all," Craig said, pointing to the M-16, "those things have been known to hurt people."

They all nodded, supporting oversized grins. "They have killed far more of us than we have them. The Jews have murdered 68 of our people in Bethlehem alone, many young boys."

"They fight with your guns," one of the Jihad members said defiantly. "They kill us with tanks, F-16s, and Apache gunships."

The tanks the Israelis made themselves, as they did the M-16s, under license from America. They would have liked to have made their own fighter jets, too, but the U.S. insisted they buy American.

"America is the only solution." The Islamic Jihad members were taking turns. "You Americans need to learn how to hold the bat."

"Hold the bat?" Craig asked.

"Yes. Rather than beat us with it, you need to learn how to hold it in the middle. You need to understand our problems."

"Why? Why are Hamas', Islamic Jihad's, and al-Qaeda's problems America's problems? Why should we care?"

"We all have many members in America. Mazook is the head of Hamas. He lives in America."

"Why doesn't America support our people or understand our problems?" the al-Qaeda terrorist asked. "They only support Israel."

"It's because Israel is the only democracy in the region. Every Arab nation is ruled by a totalitarian government. America sides with freedom, with democracies. We were against Russia when they were communists and supportive when they became a democracy. We also share common values with Israel—freedom of speech, freedom of religion, and freedom of the press. There are no such freedoms in any Arab Muslim nation. That's why America supports Israel."

The assembled had no preset response to that explanation. The Jihad members were silent as the Hamas gunman began quoting sayings in Arabic. We were told by Mahmoud that they were from Muhammad's speeches. They were growing more irritated which, considering who was holding the guns, was not a good thing.

"If you want us to hold the bat in the middle, understand your problems, and support your cause, why did Muslim militants fly those planes into the World Trade Center? Why do you hate us?"

It probably wasn't the best question I could have asked.

"You deserved it," the al-Qaeda member shot back in a tone that conveyed his hostility.

"Your government's policies caused it to happen." The Jihad members were in agreement.

"We have no quarrel with the American people, only the government," Mr. Hamas said, still stroking his rifle.

My blood began to boil. "In America," I said, "the people are the government. And second, there were no government officials in the World Trade Center—just innocent people. Why did you kill them? Why was it important to you to kill American civilians?"

"We don't hate Americans. We hate American military."

"To my knowledge," I said, "there were no military personnel in the World Trade Center."

"Yes," he said, "but the World Trade Center is the center of the economy and the economy pays the government and the government pays the military and the military murders our children."

"Hold it," I said, "When has the United Sates military murdered children?"

"In Somalia and Iraq," said the al-Qaeda member.

In frustration, I shook my head and said, "You mean to tell me that you believe American military personnel get on airplanes and fly half-way around the world for the express purpose of killing little children."

"Yes," he said.

"Why do you think they would do that?"

"So you can test your weapons and show how well they work, so you can sell them to other people who want to kill us."

I looked at Craig and said, "Wow, it sure is hard to argue with good logic."

I turned back to al-Qaeda and asked, "Where do you hear this garbage?"

He said, "It's not garbage; it's on television. I have seen it with my own eyes. I was trained by al-Qaeda in the Sudan and in Somalia. I was headed to Afghanistan before the bombings. They sent me here, to Palestine, instead."

Dumbfounded, Craig laughed out loud at the absurdity of the charge. As he did, the Palestinian said that he was not alone in his belief. He said that all Palestinians believed as he did. It was the only rational explanation as to why the bombings ultimately hurt the Palestinians more than the Jews. He said that every time Israel needed an excuse to roll tanks into Palestinian areas, they would tell the Shin Bet to direct Hamas to send out another suicide bomber.

Craig spoke up, "Let me tell you the truth. When we landed here in Israel I was greeted by a nation in mourning. The Shin Bet had sent a missile into a car, killing a Hamas leader, but also killing a small child riding with him. This brought all the people I met with to their knees, nearly to tears. Nothing could be farther from the truth."

"It is what we see. It is what we believe. In Gaza recently the Israelis targeted a group of innocent little girls on their way to school. They murdered them."

"You're saying that Israeli soldiers specifically sought out little girls and shot them in cold blood?"

"Yes."

"What I see is just the opposite. I see Americans and Jews saddened when innocents are injured. I see your people celebrate. The coffins of suicide bombers responsible for killing Jewish children are marched down the streets with great celebration." Craig was not making friends. He was clearly putting us in harm's way. I leaned over and whispered into his ear, "Craig, don't tee off the guy with the gun."

Uncomfortable with the direction the discussion had gone, Mahmoud suggested a cup of tea. At 6' 5" and nearly 300 pounds, the request appeared out of character. But then again, character was in very short supply. Mahmoud asked one of his bodyguards to bring in some tea while the terrorists settled down.

-35-

TEA WITH TERRORISTS

It was all so surreal. An elegantly flowered china tea set with matching cups was brought down into the basement on an elegant tray.

Craig continued to ask questions, but Mahmoud simply ignored him, focusing on serving the tea instead. He knew the conversation had gotten out of hand, too heated for anyone's good.

"He's ignoring me," Craig said to the terrorists. "I don't think our friend Mahmoud can do more than one thing at a time."

The big man just smiled. The others laughed.

"Would you like one lump or two?" the taller of the Islamic Jihad members asked me as he held the silver sugar spoon above the ceramic bowl.

"Two, thank you."

As Mahmoud had hoped, the tea had a quieting effect on the room.

Sipping my tea, I asked the same question I asked the Fatah captain earlier. "If you could have this land, a vibrant economy, or autonomy over where you live, which would you prefer?"

Once again, this question stirred a lively debate. Once again, the answer was the same.

"We want our land." The answer came from the Islamic Jihad. The others nodded.

"Why is it your land?" I asked.

"Because it is mentioned seven times in the Quran."

Not surprisingly, this response came from the religious terrorist, Mr. Hamas.

"It's mentioned 2,000 times in the Jewish Bible and twice that many times in the Christian Bible, so why isn't it our land? We'll keep it and you can come visit."

"I won't translate that statement." Mahmoud said to me. "Why don't you have some more tea?"

"This is our holy land. The prophet flew here on his night's journey. It belongs to us."

By that logic, I thought, every place that Patton visited should belong to America.

"Muhammad told us that owning a piece of Jerusalem was important. According to our religion, any land that we have occupied is our land. We will always fight for our land. He told us to fight for our land."

"Why fight with suicide bombers? Why do they do it?"

"There are 70 virgins waiting for us in paradise. It is our just reward."

The "us" was of concern to me. So was "our." As was the twinkle in the terrorist's eye. But nothing was as chilling as the man's smile—a serene thin smile, almost giddy. It screamed he was ready, even eager, to die.

For Mr. Hamas, paradise was calling; the virgins were whispering his name, motioning for him to slip into their lair. It was all so real to him. He faded inward, seeing himself in their midst. The conversation stalled. His eyes glazed.

This was an uncomfortable time in the room. Craig and I looked at each other and prayed silently.

The Islamic version of paradise was obviously entirely different than the Christian's view of heaven. Paradise for these disturbed souls was a place of great sexual exploitation, a fleshly world of exotic fantasies. I had heard such things but seeing and hearing them from one on the cusp of the illusion was mortifying.

"It is our reward for fighting the infidels, for martyrdom." The more diminutive member of Islamic Jihad spoke when no one else was willing.

"You cannot blame him for being hostile, for feeling as he does. The Israelis recently beat his brother. He is angry and seeks revenge. In Islam, it is part of his religion to avenge the death or beating of another. It is not like Christianity where one is asked to turn the other cheek."

Looking at his friend sympathetically, Mahmoud continued, "His father was also beaten," Mahmoud told us, pointing to the terrorist seated to our right. "He, too, is seeking revenge. It will burn inside of him until it is satisfied."

"So their Islamic faith requires them to kill—a life for a life. As I understand it, the Israelis say the same thing. Who shot first? Does anyone remember?" Craig asked, looking at Mahmoud and then canvassing the faces of the assembled mob.

Again, we knew the answer. Again, the terrorists remained silent. They knew as well. The moment the UN resolution was passed awarding the Jews five percent—as much land as the French and British had given the Arabs—the Arabs attacked. They began an unprovoked massacring of Jews. They had spilled blood first.

So as not to spill any on the green table, Craig shifted gears. He had no desire to be their latest victim.

"Before the Oslo Accords, the Palestinians were the freest and most prosperous Arabs in the world. You must know that there is not a single Arab nation, with the exception of a couple that float on oceans of black gold, that have a prosperous economy. Why do you covet this land and statehood over a decent life for your people, a life worth living?"

The giant Mahmoud nervously translated the question.

"If we have our own land and our own state, we will make our own economy," one of the Islamic Jihad members agreed with him.

"That's not consistent with the facts. At Oslo, you were given autonomy over cities like Ramallah, Bethlehem, Jericho, and Gaza. The Israelis removed their police protections and the PA was put in charge. Autonomy has brought only poverty and violence to your people. Why do you want more of these things?"

"I do not wish to translate this," Mahmoud said.

"I want you to. Please..." Craig motioned in the direction of the al-Qaeda members.

"We are suffering because the Israelis have cheated on the Oslo Accords," the terrorist answered, absolving himself and his people of responsibility.

"How has their cheating hurt your economy?"

"They built tunnels under Jerusalem when they were not supposed to. They built new settlements on our land, and did not expand our borders."

"I can understand how some of these things might make you angry, but how do they impact your economy?"

That stumped the stars. They tried a different tactic following an Arabic discussion among themselves.

"The reason is because they have blockaded our borders. There are no tourists."

"I was not questioned as I came through the check-point. The reason that there are no tourists here is that there are no tourists anywhere. Your intifada caused that. You have bombed our buildings, poisoned our people with anthrax, and killed Jews with suicide bombers. That tends to discourage tourists."

"We had to call intifada."

"Why? And is its purpose to kill Jews and Americans?"

"Yes, they occupy our land. We had no choice. Sharon marched into Al Aska mosque with 10,000 troops. Intifada was called by Arafat the next day. They are radi-cal—the Likud party and the Shaz—the black hats."

"He marched into your mosques, you say? Why would he go into el Aska? It is of no significance to the Jews."

"He went into the Dome of the Rock." Obviously the terrorists were making this up as they went along.

"Are you sure?"

"Well, he went onto the Temple Mount to prove Muslims were under his control."

"Isn't the Temple Mount the holiest place in the world for Jews? It's called the Temple Mount, not the Mosque Mount, because it was where Solomon's temple was built."

"More tea. We need more tea," Mahmoud pleaded. "Please," he said, "Do not go there. They have the guns."

"After the intifada there is no longer any reasonable chance for a peaceful settlement. Both sides have become hardened by the killing." Craig demonstrated his point visually by pounding his closed fists together. "What now?"

"More killing, if that is what it takes. We will never

give up. We will always fight for our land."

Another spoke up, "They also ended our jobs. 250,000 Palestinian jobs were taken away."

"Imagine that," Craig said, "You start killing their women and children with suicide bombers and they don't want you to work for them anymore."

They ignored the affront. "They need us and we need them. We need their jobs and they need us to do their work."

"If you get total independence, there will be less freedom of movement when you are left to police yourselves, not more. I do not know if the Jews will put the walls around you or around them, but there will be walls. I can assure you of that."

"They have stolen our water."

"The majority of the water Israelis use comes from the watershed around the Sea of Galilee and from the slopes of the Golan Heights. How is this yours?"

They just stared at Craig. This wasn't as much fun as they expected. They had become accustomed to the press letting them bellyache. They didn't like being challenged.

"They have expanded their settlements."

"They do so on top of rocky hills, not on arable land. How does this hurt your economy?"

There was no answer, only animosity, so Craig continued. "Who provides you with electricity, fresh water, roads, and the gas you put in your cars? Whose currency are you using?"

"When we are independent we will do it all ourselves."

"With no economy, how will you build and create these things?" Craig wanted to know, but didn't care to ask.

The Palestinians simply returned to their tale of woe. "They have bombed our hotels. The Jews have ransacked others. All for what?" the Al-Qaeda member asked. "Just because we shot our M-16s and Kalisnikofs into some of their homes. They were very far away. How much damage can be done by an M-16 at the range of 500 meters?"

"Who lives in those houses you were shooting at?" Craig asked politely.

"Israeli families."

"Do they have children?"

"Yes, I suppose."

"When you aim for the windows, don't you think that there's a chance you might kill them?"

"Very few. Less than six have died from this shooting. It is not an excuse to roll tanks into our cities."

"I thought you said you bought these rifles to protect yourselves. Isn't that what they are doing?"

They didn't answer, so Craig posed another question. "Will you accept responsibility for any of your problems? Or is everything the fault of the Jews and the Americans?"

Mahmoud let out a heavy sigh.

Craig began arguing with the religious Hamas member about Muhammad and I thought that he was going to call Muhammad a pervert and a pedophile. I reached over and squeezed his shoulder very hard. I said, "Craig, it is dark and time for us to leave." He said, "Just a minute, I want to finish this."

-36-

A HURRIED FAREWELL

There was a lot of Arabic chatter going on behind me. Just then, Mahmoud said, "We've got trouble, they don't think you are writers. They think you are with the CIA."

"Tell them…"

"I already have," Mahmoud interrupted. "It's past time we get you out of here. I will call the car."

This time, I reached over and got Craig by the collar of his jacket, lifted him up from his chair and said, "Craig, watch my lips, it's time for us to go now."

"Oh," he said, "Ok."

We followed Mahmoud out the door. An uneasy alliance also followed. In silence, Al-Qaeda, Islamic Jihad, Hamas, a former member of Force 17, and some American writers in disguise milled about in the darkness.

The arriving van provided little relief. The taller of the two Jihad terrorists jumped into the car with us, along with his AK 47. The other three Muslim brothers, guns in tow, hopped into a chase car as we all made our way into the darkness. We looked up and saw a reddish moon, a crescent hanging low in the sky. "How appropriate," Craig said as it began to rain.

The silence was deafening as both vans sped through the deserted and potholed streets of Bethlehem. In a confusing mix of right and left turns they made their way up and down the hilly town, past cratered buildings and barricaded homes.

In front of the only open store, the lead van, the one carrying us, stopped. Mahmoud shook my hand and got out. As he did, the accompanying member of Islamic Jihad did the same. A new driver emerged, said nothing, and drove away. I looked back, and the chase car was gone. I knew we were within moments of the border. My heart pounded in my chest.

Then I saw it off in the distance—the lights of Jerusalem. The border was less than two minutes away. The street was now cratered where tanks had recently passed. Power lines were down. This was clearly a war zone.

Speeding along the rim of an exposed canyon, the van made a series of abrupt turns. Finally, we saw it; no man's land was less than a half mile ahead. The driver eased forward then stopped abruptly. He motioned for us to get out.

Fearing that we were going to be shot in the back before reaching the relative safety of Israel, we hurried as fast as our tired legs would carry us. I thought back to the experiences, scenes, and conversations of the last four hours and wondered if there was ever a chance for peace between the Israelis and the Palestinians. The answer was no—not without God's intervention or the second coming of the Messiah.

There was Ido, waiting in his van, a pile of cigarette butts on the street beside his car.

I said, "Ido, I thought you quit smoking."

"I did," he said, "but I was so worried about you, I started again."

On the way to the Abu Gosh restaurant, where we were going to debrief each other, I said, "Craig, I just thought of a name for our book."

He said, "Tell me."

I said, "Tea with Terrorists."

Six weeks later, my heart skipped a beat when I read that Daniel Pearl was doing the same type of interview as Craig and I did and got his head cut off on international television.

I don't know what we accomplished by the trip into hell, but I did confirm what I suspected. These people will not be satisfied until every Jew and Christian in the world is eliminated.

In 2005, the Government of Israel decided to remove all Jewish settlements and Jewish people from Gaza, essentially giving the Arabs what they demanded in exchange for peace with Israel. Israel still furnishes Gaza with electricity, water, and telephone service at no cost. It's the humanitarian thing to do.

The Palestinians rewarded Israel's humanitarian actions with 5,000 or more rockets fired into Israeli civilian areas.

Craig was right when he said that walls would go up. Israel has built walls to keep suicide bombers from entering. It is working. Now the world media is decrying that Palestinians are denied free access to jobs in Israel. Such a shame.

Of the eight terrorists we interviewed that night in Bethlehem, five were killed less than two years after our meeting and two were incarcerated. One is in jail in Cypress and one in maximum security in Israel. Six months ago, the Fatah captain, who bragged to us about killing 11 Jews as they got off of a bus, was tracked down in a refugee camp. He chose not to be arrested. His funeral was celebrated by the people in the camp. They considered him a hero and a martyr.

PART 4

REFLECTIONS

Top – Super Conference in the Vines Center
Left – Falwell speaking at LU Convocation
Right – Ron Godwin
Bottom – Duke speaking at Gate Keepers Luncheon

-37-

MUSIC MINISTRY

B ack home, Liberty University and Thomas Road Baptist Church were experiencing unprecedented growth. One of the areas specifically affected by the growth was the music ministry.

Jerry Falwell first met Charles Billingsley in Jacksonville, Florida, at the annual Pastor's Conference at First Baptist Church. Homer Lindley and Jerry Vines were co-pastors at FBC for many years. The Jacksonville conference was actually inaugurated before Dr. Vines joined the staff. Under Jerry Vines' leadership, it became the largest such meeting in the country. Many times, the conference had a larger attendance than the annual meeting of the Southern Baptist Conference. Jerry Vines was Dr. Falwell's best friend in the ministry.

Because Jerry was always one of the main speakers at the Jacksonville Pastor's Conference, we got to see and hear just about every great preacher and every great singer and musician in America. In 1997, just before Jerry was to speak, we heard a young man sing a song that brought the more than 10,000 people to their feet clapping and shouting for glory. He had blond hair, a baby face and was built like a football player. We found out later that he went to college on a football scholarship as a running back.

During the song, Jerry leaned over and whispered in my ear, "Get him to come to Thomas Road for a service as soon as his schedule permits."

Charles Billingsley came for a Sunday morning service

and stayed to do a concert that night. Wow, what a talent. Jerry and our whole congregation loved him. We invited him to perform at TRBC and Liberty University every time his schedule permitted. He was very busy and in demand everywhere. Jerry's speaking schedule was filled almost every week with conferences and conventions. Before long, Charles was being scheduled for the same events. We used to joke about the *Jerry and Charles Show* being on the road again. We all became great friends.

A couple of years later, Jerry was asked to be the final speaker at a conference in rural Alabama and Charles was the invited musician. There were about 2,000 people in attendance.

The night was magic. Charles brought the house down. When Jerry was introduced, the crowd was so pumped that he had to bring them down from the ceiling. He brought the crowd to their feet a number of times, cheering him. Wow, what a night. We finally left the church and drove back to the airport where the plane was waiting to take us back to Lynchburg.

When we got on the airplane, I said to Jerry, "Doc, you know Mike Speck is thinking about leaving us early and moving back to Nashville." Mike had been our Minister of Music at TRBC for about 18 months. When he came, it was understood that he would serve for two years or less.

Jerry said, "I know, why?"

"Well," I said, "I know who your next Praise and Worship leader should be."

"Who?" he asked.

"Charles Billingsley," I answered. Jerry laughed and said, "You'll never get him. He is the hottest thing in

Charles Billingsley at Thomas Road Baptist Church

gospel music in the country. He is constantly in demand. I doubt he would even consider being full time in a church."

I said, "I may have an angle you haven't thought of."

"Have at it," he said, "You have my blessing."

Two weeks later, Carlene and I were in Atlanta on business and I called Charles and invited him and his wife, Shae, to Ruth's Chris Steak House for dinner. They accepted and met us there. This was the first time we had met Shae.

We had a nice dinner and after dessert, I asked, "Shae, when was the last time you sat in a Sunday church service and held your husband's hand?"

The question took her by surprise. She hesitated and then said, "Well, he has been traveling and singing since the day I met him. It may be that I have never done that."

I said, "How would you like to hold his hand in a service three out of every four Sundays and have your two boys sitting beside you?"

Without hesitation, she answered, "Tell me what you have in mind."

I began telling her of Dr. Falwell's dream and proposal for Charles to become the permanent Praise and Worship leader at Thomas Road Baptist Church. The plan also meant that Charles could help to establish a Praise and Worship Institute at Liberty University, ultimately training and teaching thousands of future Praise and Worship leaders and musicians. Charles was also hearing this for the first time.

I continued, "Charles could take one Sunday per month to go to some of the big churches and also do concert tours occasionally during the week."

"This sounds great," she said. "But wait a minute, does that mean I have to move to Lynchburg? I can't do that. My mother lives only two hours away in Birmingham. My dad is in Atlanta and Charles' parents live here, too. I can't move away to a little town that I've never even been to."

To that point, Charles hadn't said a word. Carlene said to Shae, "I know how you feel. We had always lived in big cities; Houston, Atlanta, Charlotte, and we always fought it when Jerry tried to talk us into moving to Lynchburg. We thought we would be bored stiff in such a tiny town, but we love it."

"Shae," I said, "Charles is scheduled to be in Lynchburg in two weeks. He is singing and leading worship at Thomas Road on Sunday morning, performing a concert Sunday night and singing at Liberty's convocation on Monday morning. If you will come with him, we'll send our plane to pick up both of you on Friday and let you spend Saturday and Sunday getting to know the city and the people—and maybe start looking for a house while you are at it."

"Ok, I'll come," she said, "but I don't think I will ever agree to move."

I looked at Charles and said, "While you are there, you, Jerry, and Jonathan need to talk about the details." He just smiled.

It took a few months to work out all of the details and for God to work in Shae's heart. In the spring of 2002, the Billingsleys became a part of the Jerry Falwell extended family.

Charles was instrumental in putting together the staff, faculty, and the curriculum for Jerry's dream Praise and Worship Institute. Scott Bullman was the first person Charles brought on board. Scott leads our 300-voice choir and teaches in the Institute. Vernon Whaley is now the Dean of the Institute and has over 400 students and scores of graduates serving in churches around the nation. Another one of Jerry Falwell's dreams lives on.

-38-

A TIME FOR TESTING

When we moved to Lynchburg in 1992, although we had never lived there, it was almost like coming home. After working out of Lynchburg for many years, we had built so many great friendships. We were welcomed with open arms.

The frenzied days of the Moral Majority were behind us and Liberty had its own TV studio and satellite uplink right on campus. Jerry was still a regular guest on many television programs, but now he could do those interviews from Lynchburg instead of having to travel to Washington or New York so much.

Our TV crew was always on alert. Sometimes we would have less than an hour's notice to put together the crew, be up on the satellite, and be on the air.

He appeared on television from Lynchburg sometimes five times a week. Occasionally, he would travel to New York or Washington or even Los Angeles to do television or speak.

Jerry was spending almost all of his time and energy in growing Liberty University. The adverse effects of the moral failures of Jim Bakker and Jimmy Swaggart left many good and effective gospel ministries in financial difficulties. The Old Time Gospel Hour was not immune.

The Old Time Gospel Hour was the entity that was responsible for raising money to fund the operation of all aspects of the Jerry Falwell Ministries. That included the Liberty Broadcasting Network, Elim Home for alcoholics, Godparent Home for unwed mothers, World Missions, the Lynchburg Christian Academy and Liberty University.

After the Bakker and Swaggart incidences, the income from our television donors dropped by about 25% overnight. Jerry could cut back the spending at many of the organizations, but the university was different. He could not tell 4,000 students to all go home and that we would call when we got the finances worked out. He felt he had to work his way out of the mess while keeping the university in operation. That dug the financial hole deeper.

The ministry had plenty of assets so he decided on a

tax free educational bond issue, a program that allowed many other schools to finance growth; schools like Notre Dame, Brigham Young and Regent University. The ACLU filed suit against it, claiming separation of church and state. They ultimately prevailed in court.

Jerry decided to issue taxable bonds. A major insurance company contracted to complete the transaction and then defaulted at the very last minute. The time and expense of those efforts left the ministry in a major financial crisis.

Jerry met with the creditors and worked out an agreement describing all would be paid in a certain period of time. That was a great day when he was out from under the immediate pressure. However, the debt was still there and had to be paid and the growing university still had to be operated.

Jerry determined to go to the Bible for wisdom and courage. After a period of time in the Word and prayer, he told me that he was going on a 40-day fast—fasting and praying for God to do something miraculous.

He said that he was asking for something so gigantic that if it was successful, everyone would know that only God could have made it happen.

I was with him the whole time during the fast. He really fasted. Lunch on the 41st day was at McDonalds. Three weeks later, Jerry said to me, "I was fasting and asking for God to do something miraculous and he did. He did it in my life. I am going on another 40-day fast to ask Him specifically for the needs of Liberty University."

Twenty-two days after his first 40-day fast, he began another identical 40-day regimen. About 30 days into this fast, I jokingly said to him, "Doc, I wish you would go back to eating. You get mean when you're hungry."

During that 102 day period, Jerry never lost his energy or stamina, but he did lose 75 pounds. That was an amazing time in his life and also mine. I saw a totally different Jerry Falwell than the world saw. I saw a man wholly committed to God's will and committed to expanding his original vision to include even more incredible dreams and goals.

-39-

A TIME FOR GROWTH

Things began to happen at Liberty. A small amount of the debt was forgiven and one of our truest friends bought some of the debt and forgave it. For the first time since the Bakker–Swaggart scandal, things were moving in the right direction.

Because of our financial difficulties, Liberty was placed on academic probation by the Southern Association of Colleges and Schools. Losing our accreditation would have been devastating for the university. Mending that probation problem was a top priority for Jerry and the entire university staff.

John Borek was recruited as a consultant to guide Liberty through the process of restoration. He not only was successful in getting Liberty off probation but he guided it through its 10 year reaffirmation. Liberty University had arrived and took its place alongside other vibrant and growing educational institutions. Jerry always felt that God brought John to Liberty for this purpose.

Liberty's DeMoss Learning Center and The Vines Center Arena
John Borek became President of the university.

With the accreditation issue behind him, Jerry Falwell still had the problem of day-to-day operating funds. During this period, the growth of the student body began to plateau. For the first time, the incoming freshman class was smaller than the freshman class of the previous year. Jerry Falwell determined not to let this be a trend. He turned to Rod Godwin.

Ron was the Executive Director of the Moral Majority until 1984, when he left to help create the Washington Times Newspaper. The paper became one of the great conservative voices in the nation. After 11 years at the Times, he left to create other companies, made them profitable, and sold them.

He came to Lynchburg to visit and was convinced by Jerry to stay. He took over the presidency of Jerry Falwell Ministries and made it profitable.

Ron Godwin was the best people manager that I had ever met. Jerry always said that he had a personality like barbed-wire so he was not a great people person. Ron and I became best of friends. We had a common goal. Our collective purpose was to serve Jerry Falwell.

Jerry decided to take over the recruitment of new students and made Ron his point man. That was a magic combination. The freshman class was 1,460 students the semester before Jerry and Ron began their campaign. The next semester, 2,640 students registered for the incoming class. That's an 80% increase in one year. Ron also made marketing the Distance Learning Program a major priority.

Ron put together management teams that were given specific projects and time schedules. Each team leader was held accountable for the progress of his project and was required to give progress reports at strict intervals. That reporting requirement was what brought accountability and accountability is what brought success.

Jerry and Ron had finally found the way out of the financial swamp and they were totally consumed with making it work. They decided to grow Liberty out of debt. Liberty began a growth curve that has continued until this very day.

Jerry was constantly remembering his 40-days of prayer and fasting. He always felt that every good thing that happened came from God because of those days.

About this time, God began to open the windows of heaven and blessings began to surge from all sides. Many things happened at about the same time.

It was announced in a board meeting that Arthur L. Williams had made a commitment to give a gift of $4.5 million dollars to the university if we could raise a matching amount. Two of our longtime board members, Tim and Beverly LaHaye, spoke up and said, "We will give the same amount toward the building of a student activities building."

Jerry commissioned me to meet with an architect to

The Ericsson Building

begin designing the activities building and the Athletic Director began working to design the Arthur L. Williams football operations building.

About the same time, the Swedish-owned Ericsson Company decided to sell all of their North American real estate holdings and move their cellular telephone manufacturing operations to Asia. The Lynchburg, Virginia, facility was built by the General Electric Company in the 1950's and later sold to Ericsson. The entire property consisted of 880,000 square feet of pristine offices, a plant, warehouse, and 113 acres of land with a replacement value of over $100 million dollars. The most important aspect of it was that it was contiguous to the 4,500-acre Liberty University campus.

Over the years that I worked with Jerry, I heard him say enumerable times that one day God would give us that property.

The property was going to be auctioned to the highest bidder in December of 2004. Jerry wanted to offer a certain amount. Jerry Jr. offered $500 more than his dad told him. His reasoning was, if someone else bid the same amount, we would still be the highest bidder.

The bids were opened on December 10 and, miraculously, we were the highest bidder by $500. Jerry Jr. was the hero. The closing was set for February 14, 2005, just 64 days later. Jerry Jr. arranged for a bridge loan until we could determine how we would pay for the property.

-40-

BLESSINGS AND BUILDINGS

In the second week of January, I received a call from Jack Eggar, the president of AWANA, a major ministry headquartered in Chicago, Illinois. He told me that a large company had purchased a building in the Chicago area with the intent of giving it to AWANA, but at the last minute, his board turned it down.

He continued by saying, "One of my best friends from college days is Jerry Thorpe." Thorpe was a member of the Board of Trustees at Liberty. Eggar said, "When I told Jerry Thorpe that my board refused the gift, he asked, 'Why don't you ask the company to give the building to Liberty University? They will surely take it and do something important with it.'"

"So," Eggar said, "I called the company with that request, and they said they would give it to Liberty."

I took his number and went into Dr. Falwell's office and gave him the information. He picked up the telephone and called Jack Eggar immediately. He told Jack that he would come to Chicago later that week. I made all of the arrangements and Jerry, Ron Godwin, and I flew into the Elgin Illinois Airport. Jack met us and took us directly to the building.

The 3-story building had 300,000 square feet of floor space and undercover parking for 1,000 cars, sitting on 80 acres of land next to a major highway. Six months after the building was completed and occupied, the company was lost in a hostile takeover, the building was emptied, and everyone was either fired or moved to Georgia. The new owners sold off the assets and placed the company into bankruptcy. The building was put up for sale.

Hobby Lobby, a retail arts and crafts company with about 350 outlet stores, is owned and operated by a family with strong Christian faith and principles. They are headquartered in Oklahoma City. Over the years, they have developed a model of giving to Christian ministries and churches that involves purchasing buildings and eventually giving those buildings to a ministry to be used in the Lord's work.

Hobby Lobby was the company that purchased the building and property and was ready to give it to AWANA.

Jerry, Ron, and I inspected every inch of the building. It was impressive. We took pictures. We had lunch with Jack and his family and returned to Lynchburg late that afternoon.

At this point, the closing on the Ericsson property was only four weeks away.

Jerry tried his best to find a legitimate use for the building in Chicago, but his goal had always been to centralize everything in Lynchburg. He wanted to be able to see and touch all aspects of the ministry.

On February 12 (just two days before the Ericsson closing) over lunch, Jerry made the decision to tell the owners of Hobby Lobby how much we appreciated the offer but there was just no justifiable purpose for us to have a building in Chicago. He wanted to suggest that they give the building to James McDonald who was pastor of a 6,000-member church in Chicago and was looking for a piece of property so they could relocate.

I reminded Jerry that he would be speaking in St. Louis the next night (February 13) and suggested that we leave early, fly to Oklahoma City first and meet David Green, the owner of Hobby Lobby, and thank him personally. Jerry agreed that it was a good idea. When we returned to our offices, I called and set the meeting with Mr. Green for 10:00 a.m. the next morning. I scheduled a 7:00 a.m. departure.

Later in the day, I went to Jerry and asked him if he understood Hobby Lobby's giving model and exactly how it worked. He answered no.

I said, "Neither do I, but here is a way for us to find out. Tomorrow, after you get to know David Green a little better, I think you should say, 'I wish I had met you a few months ago.' He will say, 'Why is that?' You should say, 'Because we have a project in Lynchburg that might fit your giving model.' Mr. Green will say, 'Really, what is it?' Then I will pull the Ericsson plans from my briefcase and let's just see where it goes."

When Jerry said to Mr. Green, "I wish I had met you a few months ago," everyone followed the script perfectly. After he looked at the plans for a few minutes, Mr. Green asked Jerry if he had closed on the sale yet. Jerry said, "We were supposed to close tomorrow morning at 9:00 a.m.,

but Jerry Jr., my son and our in-house council called me
just as we landed and told me that the Ericsson attorneys
were hung up in a snow storm in Boston and could not be
in Lynchburg until the 19th. That is six days from now."

David Green asked a few questions about the selling
price and details of the property. He asked to be excused
for a couple of minutes and left the room. When he
returned in about 10 minutes, he said, "Jerry, why don't I
buy this and give it to you?"

Jerry was stunned. He immediately called Jerry Jr. and
introduced him to David Green and his attorney. David
said, "You guys work out the details." And they did.

Jerry Jr. had 5 days until closing. All of the closing
documents were already completed but they were between
Ericsson and Thomas Road Baptist Church, a non-profit
organization. The new closing documents had to be
between Ericsson and Hobby Lobby, a for-profit corpora-
tion. Much of the language had to be altered and vetted
by Ericsson, Hobby Lobby, and TRBC's attorneys.

Jerry Jr. drove the attorneys to the point of exhaustion
to get it all done. By February 19 at 9:00 a.m., all was
complete and signed. Jerry Jr. was the hero again.

Through David Green and Hobby Lobby, God gave
the Ericsson property to Thomas Road Baptist Church,
just like Jerry told me He would.

Instead of building a new building to house the
LaHaye Student Activities Center, we were able to incor-
porate the NCAA regulation size pool, 5 regulation size
basketball courts, exercise, aerobics and weight lifting
rooms in the new North Campus (the former Ericsson
building). The LaHaye's $4.5 million dollar donation paid
not only for the construction, but it equipped everything.

Williams Football Stadium

Arthur Williams' donation went to build the Football Operations center.

A large portion of the old Ericsson building was allotted to Liberty Christian Academy. A few months later, we broke ground for the new 6,000-seat sanctuary of Thomas Road Baptist Church. The church building was a new structure and was built adjacent to the academy so the classes could be doubly used as school classrooms and Sunday school classrooms.

July 2, 2006 was the 50th anniversary of the founding of Thomas Road Baptist Church and the first service in our new sanctuary. More than 10,000 people attended. Also, because it was the celebration day of the 203rd birthday of the United States, we had a huge patriotic celebration and giant fireworks display that afternoon and evening in the Liberty University football stadium. We tried to count the number of people who came and lost count at 30,000.

Jerry Falwell was a visionary of gigantic proportions. Unlike the vast majority of visionaries, he was personally able to see his visions and dreams fulfilled. I think it was Voltaire who said, "Some people see the world as it is and ask 'Why?' Others see the world as it could be and ask, 'Why Not?'" With the latter statement, I think Voltaire was looking 400 years in the future and talking about Jerry Falwell.

In 50 years, under Jerry's leadership, Thomas Road Baptist Church raised and spent more than $5 billion dollars and established:

- Elim Home for drug and alcohol addicted men,

- Old Time Gospel Hour television program, which was the longest continuously running religious television program in the world,

- Liberty Christian Academy, which now has about 2,000 students,

- Liberty Godparent Home, a home for unwed mothers,

- Liberty University, the largest distinctively Christian university in the world, with a total enrollment of 50,000 students,

- Thousands of churches have been planted around the world,

- More than 3 million people who have written that they came to faith in Christ as a result of one of the ministry outreaches.

The day Jerry Falwell died, Liberty had sufficient funds in a debt account to completely eradicate the remaining debt.

-41-

ILLNESS

One night about midnight, I was awaken by a call from David Randlet, asking if I had received a call from the hospital yet. I told him that I had not. He said, "You will. Jerry has been taken to the emergency room." As Senior Associate pastor of TRBC, David was always called when one of our church members was admitted, during the night, to the emergency room. Carlene and I dressed and drove to the Lynchburg General Hospital.

Lynchburg is a small town but it has advanced medical facilities that rival almost any place in the country, especially in the area of coronary treatment.

We found Jerry in a treatment room being attended by a staff of doctors and nurses, many who were graduates of Liberty University's nursing program. He looked pale and was obviously in pain. They were prepping him for x-rays and EKG. He seemed glad that we came. We stayed with Macel while he was going through tests.

He was admitted for observation. It was not clear whether his problem was heart related or not. Two nights later, he was feeling much better and was looking forward to going home in a day or so. While he was talking and having fun with some of the Liberty nurses, he stopped mid-sentence and said, "Someone get me a doctor now. I can't breathe." A nurse dashed out of the room and almost ran into a doctor that was walking by. He happened to be the leading pulmonary physician in Lynchburg. He did a quick examination and said, "I need you to sign an authorization for us to put you on a ventilator."

Jerry asked, "What's the alternative?"

The doctor said, "Funeral home."

"Let's do it," Jerry said. And they did. He was on the breathing apparatus for five days.

Although some of the time he seemed to be awake with the tube down his throat, he was given a medication that would not let him remember anything about this. It was a scary time for all of us. It seemed our superman was showing signs of being mortal. I received hundreds of phone calls from friends and well wishers.

He was happy when he was released from the hospital for more than one reason. Happy not only to be going home, but we learned the day before that the Lady Flames basketball team had been given an invitation to the NCAA Final 64 Tournament. Jerry was the number one Liberty

University sports fanatic.

A few days later, the Lady Flames played their first game of the tournament in Baltimore, Maryland. Jerry would not even think of not being there. They won and two days later, also in Baltimore, they won again. They had advanced to the Sweet Sixteen. Their next game was on Saturday in Chattanooga, Tennessee, against Louisiana State University, who, after defeating Liberty, went on to be crowned National Champions. Jerry looked like the head cheerleader at each of those games.

The next day was Easter Sunday. Jerry preached twice that Sunday morning.

The next night (Monday), Jerry and Macel were at home when Jerry shouted, "Macel, come quickly. Drive me to the hospital—I can't breathe."

She said, "Let me call 911."

"No," he answered, "There isn't time. You'll have to take me."

She hurried around getting her car keys, helped Jerry into the car, and raced out of the driveway toward the hospital. She finally got her cell phone out and called 911. The operator tried to get her to pull the car to the side of the road and wait for an ambulance. She said, "No, I am going to the hospital." Just as she said that, Jerry passed out and fell over on her. She used her right hand to hold him upright so she could drive. The drive from her home to the emergency room was about 15 minutes. She was terrified.

She arrived at the hospital just as four EMTs were exiting the emergency room going to their ambulances. She blew her horn and yelled, "He's not breathing. Help him—help him." The EMTs responded immediately by yanking the car door open and carrying Jerry to a nearby gurney. A doctor met them at the door and immediately checked for a pulse and found none. The doctor asked Macel how long he had been unconscious. Her answer was about 10 minutes.

While the doctor was examining Jerry, the EMTs were setting up their electric paddles, waiting for the doctor's order to shock him to get his heart beating again. It took three times, but his heart started to beat again on its own. Again, Jerry was put on a ventilator. Later that night, the doctor told Macel that she saved Jerry's life.

Jerry Jr. came to be with his mom. Jonathan was out of town with his family. We called and gave him the news about his dad. The following morning Jonathan drove to Richmond to pick up Jeannie. This time, everyone was worried.

Jerry was unconscious for three days. Thursday night he began to stir and by Friday afternoon he was able to carry on a conversation. I was in the room with him alone. After some small talk, he asked me what day it was. I told him that it was Friday. He said, "Duke, I have to get out of here. I have to preach Sunday."

I said, "Doc, number one, I don't think the doctor will let you out, and number two, if he did, Macel is not going to let you preach."

He said, "I have never missed preaching on Easter Sunday."

"Doc," I said, "Last Sunday was Easter."

He looked at me and asked, "Did I preach?"

I told him, "You not only preached twice, you did a CNN interview with Wolf Blitzer and we had a luncheon with the Ehrhorns from Colorado. After Saturday, I think you overdid it and that's why you are back in the hospital."

He said, "Saturday, what did we do Saturday?"

I said, "You don't remember Saturday? Doc, your Lady Flames basketball team went to the NCAA Sweet Sixteen."

He almost hollered, "You're kidding, was I there?"

"You were not only at that game; you were in Baltimore twice when they won those games." He had totally lost the week between his hospital stays. He never recovered them.

He was so excited he could hardly contain himself. He made me promise that I would get him a video of all the games so he could view them the next day. He was released from the hospital about a week later, but superman was not flying as high.

In retrospect, Jerry was never the same after that. For as long as I had known him, there was never a time that he did not have a development of some kind going. Jerry's last project was to move the church to Liberty Mountain. The move was completed on July 2, 2006. From then until he died 10 months later, he never began another project and, to my knowledge, he never went back to the old building. He never liked to look back.

A few months later, I went with him to the Cleveland Clinic in Ohio. The doctors installed 4 coated stents in his heart during the four day stay. Carlene and Macel met us when we arrived home on Saturday night. They both said that Jerry looked as tired and weary as they had ever seen him. He could not even walk from the plane to his car without sitting and resting. I had my doubts about his ability to preach the next morning, but he fooled me. He looked and felt good on Sunday.

-42-

GOING HOME

In 2007, I began to have pains in my lower back and went to see an orthopedic specialist. After a lot of tests and alternative treatments, it was decided that I needed spinal surgery.

Tuesday, May 15, 2007 at 10:00 a.m., Carlene and I were at the surgeon's office scheduling my surgery. Had I not been there, I would have been at breakfast with Jerry and Ron. We finished up at the doctor's office about 11:00 and decided to take an early lunch. At 11:20, my cell phone rang. It was Hollis McGarity. She worked in the Liberty Call Center, right across the parking lot from the mansion where Jerry and I had our office.

She said, "Duke, there is something bad going on at the mansion. There are fire trucks, ambulances and police cars on the lawn in front of the offices." I thanked her and dialed the number for Amanda, our receptionist.

I said, "Amanda, what's going on?"

She hesitated. I could hear voices in the background as she said, "Duke, I'll have to call you back."

I told her, "I understand, just tell me this; is it Jerry?"

She had a quiver in her voice when she answered, "Yes."

I said, "Thank you; I will meet the ambulance at the hospital."

Carlene and I left the restaurant and drove quickly to the emergency room at the hospital. We arrived as the EMTs were taking him through the door. Jonathan had ridden in the ambulance and was still holding his dad's hand. Jerry was pale and there was no movement.

Instinctively I thought he was already gone. Macel and Jerry Jr. arrived a little while after we did. Carlene sat with Macel and everyone prayed. Ron Godwin came. We were both in a state of shock. Deep down, we knew this could happen, but we were never ready.

I looked outside and saw TV satellite trucks were setting up in the parking lot of the hospital. A giant had passed from the scene and they were there to cover it. Jerry had a good relationship with the local television stations and they were just as sad as were we. They kept their distance until Ron Godwin gave them the word that Jerry Falwell had died at 12:40 p.m.

In just a short time, there were signs all over Lynchburg with messages of condolences to the Falwell family. We would see people in restaurants wearing black ribbons in remembrance of Jerry. It seemed as though the entire city was in mourning. Later that day, I needed to go to the church to pick up something and saw 10 satellite trucks in the parking lot, each with a reporter on camera.

Early the next morning I was interviewed by Fox Network and Fox News. As soon as the interview was completed, my phone began to ring with calls from all over the world. I received calls from Israel, India, Uzbekistan and all over America. People wanted me to give the message to the Falwell family that they were being uplifted in prayer.

We later learned that Jerry had visited his cardiologist the previous Thursday. The doctor wanted to put him in the hospital and do a heart catheterization with the prospect of doing by-pass surgery. Jerry said he wanted to wait. He didn't want to be in the hospital during graduation week.

Jerry, Jerry Jr., and Jonathan

The rest of the week is still a blur. Carlene and I were running on pure adrenaline. Graduation was always a busy time because we had to host many of the out of town dignitaries. This year was no different; only more hectic. Ron Godwin hosted Newt Gingrich, our commencement speaker, and I hosted a number of the people being honored by the university with degrees.

I will be forever grateful to the family for inviting Carlene and I to join them for the private family viewing at the funeral home. Jerry looked just like he did when I saw him the last time. He was wearing a dark suit and a red tie.

Macel told me that she looked at more than twenty red ties in Jerry's closet befores he found one that did not have a food stain on it. That was one of the jokes we were constantly laughing about. Jerry was always eating so fast that he would drop food on his tie or suit, and I was always trying to clean it.

We stood around for about an hour and a half just reminiscing. Macel was doing better than we expected, but we knew that the realization had not totally hit her yet. There were bad days to come for all of us. The clouds were gathering.

Paul Whitten, the funeral director, was a member of our church. Paul called me aside and told me that the company that owned the funeral home also owned the one in Washington, D.C., that conducted Ronald Reagan's funeral. He told me that he contacted them that morning and asked if we could use the same funeral bier (the stand on which the casket is placed to lie in state) that was used for Ronald Reagan.

Paul knew that Reagan was Jerry Falwell's hero. They had already delivered it and it was sitting in the next room. Later Jerry was taken to the Grand Lobby at Liberty University and placed on that bier where it lay in state for three days.

Tens of thousands of people lined up to pay their

respects and give a final goodbye to a fallen pastor, states-man, champion, mentor, and friend. On Sunday after-noon, a horse drawn hearse was used to transport Jerry in a processional along a crowd lined corridor from the Grand Lobby to the sanctuary of Thomas Road Baptist Church. I've never experienced anything like it. We began to receive requests for seating at the memorial service from the far corners of the nation. Jerry had a lot of friends.

Jerry had left detailed instructions as to who he want-ed to participate in his funeral when he died. Adrian Rogers died a few months before Jerry and was the only person on his list not there. Jerry Vines and Franklin Graham were the main speakers.

Between the time of Jerry's death and his memorial service, there was a Sunday. Everyone was wondering who would preach at TRBC. The decision, of course, was left to the Falwell family. Because it was graduation weekend, there were many well-known preachers in town so we all expected one of them to be chosen. Jonathan was never in doubt about who would preach. In his heart, he knew it was time for him to step up. This was a right-of-passage for him and he would rise to the occasion. And he did.

The building was filled to overflowing when Jonathan told us, "When Moses died, Joshua was the one God chose to lead His people."

He continued by saying, "Today our Moses is gone and each one of us is Joshua." That day, a true leader was inau-gurated.

A few weeks later, the deacons met and officially named Jonathan pastor of Thomas Road Baptist Church. In the first year, more than 4,000 people (including chil-dren) became members of the church. We baptized more than 1,500.

Jerry Jr. became Chancellor and President of Liberty University. The growth curve established by Jerry Sr. and Ron Godwin continues to this day. The succession plan that Jerry envisioned became a reality and was seamless. Both young men have carved out a niche of their own.

I waited more than two years after Jerry's death to write this book. Macel wrote her book about Jerry as a husband. Jonathan wrote about Jerry as a father. I wanted to write about Jerry as a best friend.

For 38 years, I served him in different capacities. I was there when he began to articulate the dream. Others may have laughed; I didn't because I wanted to go along for the ride. What a ride it was.

In my estimation, Jerry Falwell was the greatest man of vision the world has ever known. You can be a great man of vision only if you are a great man of prayer. Every fulfilled dream was first bathed in prayer. His answered prayers are legion and as a result, his legacy will take a place of honor in the history books.

I said earlier that Jerry was never without the dream of another project in his mind just bursting to get out. After he moved Thomas Road Baptist Church to Liberty Mountain, he never started another project. He died 10 months later.

I began this book with a quote from D. L. Moody—I will end it with a quote from Jerry Falwell two weeks before he died.

"God's man is indestructible until he has finished the work God has called him to do."

-43-

ACKNOWLEDGEMENTS

People go through life meeting other people and sometimes those people become friends. On rare occasions do friends become more than friends. However, each one of this cast is more than a friend. They are part of the Jerry Falwell brotherhood and will forever be in my memory.

Jerry maintained his office and that of his immediate staff in the old home place of Senator Carter Glass. Glass was a long time United States Senator and was Secretary of the Treasury under President Woodrow Wilson. The first land purchase for what is now Liberty Mountain was that mansion and the 160 acres that surrounded it.

There are three ladies that were as important to the narratives of the legacy of Jerry Falwell as anyone. They managed the mansion office and served the people working there. One day, I referred to them as angels, because they were ministering spirits. The name stuck. Each morning when I would arrive at the office, I greeted them with, "Good morning, angels."

Kathy Rusk was the head angel. She was Jerry's administrative assistant for about 25 years. When I moved to Lynchburg and took the title of Executive Assistant, she and I worked closely, coordinating the scheduling of Jerry's time and the minute details of planning his travel for out of town meetings and speaking engagements. She worked long hours without complaining one time. She was and is an incredible friend.

I called **Kelli Tripp** "magic fingers." If I was researching something for a document or letter and I needed an answer to a historical or a technical question, Kelli could find the answer on the Internet in a flash. She is Jerry Jr.'s paralegal assistant.

Amanda Stanley was the receptionist and answered the telephones for us. I told her she reminded me of a juggler, because she could keep four calls going at the same time and not make anyone angry because they never realized that she had them on hold.

Those three were the angels.

I have talked about **Ron Godwin** at length in the book. The mission Ron and I shared was to serve and assist Jerry Falwell. Never was our mission in conflict.

Edward Hindson is a great long-term friend. He is a talent without peer. I have often said, "If you need to put together a 10-part series on the significances of the Mayan Pyramids and their relationship to the book of Revelation, and began filming next Thursday, Ed Hindson is the only call you need to make." Ed is also one of the greatest pulpiteers in America. Ed, Donna, Carlene and I have traveled the world together.

Dan Reber is a Lynchburg businessman who loved Jerry Falwell and was always there when a friend was needed. He was one of the people who Jerry relied upon for business advice and counsel. Many times when immediate funds were necessary to avert disaster, Dan and Jan Reber came through.

Charles Billingsley is a dear friend and partner in the Lord's ministry. He and Jonathan Falwell make an outstanding platform team.

Benny Tate is the pastor of one of the most unusual churches I have ever attended. Rock Springs Church is about 50 miles southeast of Atlanta, Georgia. The first time I was there, it seemed as if we had driven down a country road a long way from civilization. We finally came to a clearing and saw a huge church building with acres of paved parking full of cars.

That night, about 1,800 people came to hear Ergun Caner speak. Jerry Falwell was scheduled, but that was during a time that he was in the hospital.

Benny Tate and I became instant friends. He is the president of a denomination headquartered in Jackson, Mississippi. I have spoken in his church and many of the churches in his denomination. He is a pastor that has a burning burden for souls. He personally baptizes about 350 people per year who come to faith in Christ under his preaching. There is a special friendship bond between us.

There are so many others that I could name who have had an impact on my life, but there is not enough time nor enough paper.

-44-

THANK YOU FOR THE DOCTORATE

L iberty University 2009 graduates, their friends and family filled the Worship Center at Thomas Road Baptist Church to capacity for the 2009 Baccalaureate service. Each year the Baccalaureate service is a spiritual farewell that precedes the actual commencement and graduation ceremonies the next day. That night, May 8, Liberty University honored me with a Doctor of Humanities degree.

My emotions were running in all directions that night. Jerry Jr. emailed me a month earlier and said that the Board of Liberty University had voted unanimously to confer a degree on me. I did not expect it.

Just before the Baccalaureate service, I thanked Jerry for the honor. He said, "Duke, you deserve it."

I responded, "I'm not so sure of that, but I will tell you this: you're not getting it back."

I was going to say a few words of thanks after I was hooded, but I was out of position to the microphone and would have looked awkward. In retrospect, there was not enough time to say what was on my heart, but I will give it a shot here.

Macel, Jerry Jr. & Becki, Jeannie, Jonathan & Shari, you have all been so kind to Carlene, Kim, and me. You have understood that the loss of Jerry was a demoralizing blow to me also.

Occasionally, I drive up on Liberty Mountain and

marvel at what God has done through one man. I see thousands of young people facing the future deeply submerged in the dreams and vision of Jerry. I see thousands of people who came to Christ because of Jerry's love for souls. I see families serving the Lord. These things and people are the footprints of Jerry Falwell.

There are times, when I am there, that I almost weep. Weep with sadness that my best friend is no longer here, and sometimes I weep with joy that God allowed me to be a small part of the legacy.

The dream lives on.

Inside the auditorium of the Vine Center

Aerial View of Old Thomas Road Baptist Church

Jerry Falwell and Duke